THE
COACH'S WIFE

Carolyn Allen

CAROLYN ALLEN

THE COACH'S WIFE

Carolyn Allen, The Coach's Wife

ISBN 1-887002-51-0

Cross Training Publishing
317 West Second Street
Grand Island, NE 68801
(308) 384-5762

Library of Congress Cataloging in Publication Data in Progress.

Published by Cross Training Publishing,
317 West Second Street
Grand Island, NE 68801
1-800-430-8588

DEDICATION

To Randy–
my coach, my teammate, my inspiration!

and to the memory of Scott Harrison,
a great "coach's kid."

ACKNOWLEDGMENTS

Thank you to:

All the coaches' wives who opened their hearts and told me their stories. It was like Christmas opening all the questionnaires! This book is YOUR gift to coaches' wives everywhere. Your names and schools are listed in the appendix.

Randy, who initiated the idea for this book, gave me confidence, prayed for me and encouraged me throughout. I love and respect you and am so proud to be your wife!

Zac and Ashley, for patience and support through your thrilling back-to-back senior years and into college. You each bring a constant joy and smile to my heart.

Jennie Stowers Allen, Zacs' wife, and a perfect answer to our prayers.

Debbie Harrison and Stacey Rhiddlehoover, coaches' wives on our staff for 17 and 10 years. Weve shared the sweetest years traveling and cheering for each other's children.

Cathy Jackson, Janene Pratt, Nancy Brock, Bonnie Green, Dr. Jeri Pfeifer, and Doris Moser: loyal friends and mentors. You contributed greatly with your keen insight in reviewing the manuscript.

Susan Keeling, friend and role model. You have been a light to my path.

Joe and Debbie-Jo White, for pointing me to Cross Training Publishing, and for your abiding friendship with the Allen family.

Gordon Thiessen, publisher, for your relaxed approach and belief in this project.

Kathy Edwards, for capturing the essence of the coaching life in your illustrations.

Eleanor Goen, Amy Duncan, and Emily Bryant, for excellent typing skills.

Darla Swanner, a miracle of a writer and friend. Thank you for your wisdom.

And to my family who has loved me unconditionally: Carol Jayne and Billy Crump, Onkle Al Seligman, my beloved late grandmother Carolyn Washer, Charlie and Dorothy Hildebrandt, Connie and (the late) Herman Hildebrandt, and the Allen gang (our biggest fans): Codie, Hoss, Mark, Michelle, Lane, Jake, Matt, and Hubbell.

CONTENTS

FOREWORD

I was a coach's wife for 37 seasons of my life. I loved being a football coach's wife; I loved the academic environment; I loved the association with the student athletes; and I shall always be appreciative of the fact that I had the privilege of living with a man whom I felt was called to be a coach . . . to work with young men, to mold their lives, and to prepare them for life after football.

A woman once said to me, "It must be wonderful to be married to a coach who has to work only a few hours on Saturday afternoon." Knowing that I could not begin to help her understand the complexity of my life and the life of every other coach's wife, I replied, "Yes, it is wonderful. I wish that you could be married to a coach." Little did she realize there is so much more . . . .

Carolyn Allen has touched every area of being a coach's wife. If you have a question, she has an answer. The beauty of this book is . . . though I consider Carolyn a consummate coach's wife with a great deal of wisdom . . . she offers her readers a wonderful cross-section of experience, information, and honest feelings from coaches' wives, of all ages and experience, from all over this nation.

I appreciate the fact that Carolyn has devoted an entire chapter to the importance of faith in our lives. She says, "When balancing the emotional, physical, and mental demands–a strong spiritual life can be the difference between giving up and hanging on!"

Whether you are married to a coach or to some other intense individual in another profession, you will enjoy this book, and you will be enlightened, as well.

Mrs. Grant Teaff (Donell)

INTRODUCTION

A coach's wife rarely has her husband's undivided attention. It sometimes happens when you are traveling alone as a couple on a long stretch of highway.

This was the scene a couple of years ago after Randy and I attended a Fellowship of Christian Athletes Camp. As "huddle" leaders, our lives were intertwined with our small group of eight coaching couples for 72 hours. Despite differences in age, geography, and coaching position, we all had the same passions and struggles.

Randy told me that he soon would be interviewing new coaches for his staff. He voiced the importance of the coaches wife's role. "Wouldn't it be great if there was something *written* to help coaches' wives learn from each other?" The light flashed on! We brainstormed all the way home.

With much encouragement, I sent hundreds of questionnaires to coaches' wives across the country. The response was overwhelming!

May *The Coach's Wife* broaden your perspective, deepen your appreciation, strengthen your home, and solidify your dependence on God.

Here's to *your* winning *team!*

WANT TO GO ON THIS SCOUTING TRIP
WITH ME, HONEY?

CHAPTER ONE

Early Days

It was a hot West Texas Monday in August. I left the parking lot of Bill's Superette and headed for the practice field. My husband, Randy, was beginning his second year as a head football coach. Zac, age 6, and Ashley, 4, sat in the back seat with the ice chest between them. Perfect timing! As we drove up, the players were running their final wind sprints. "Time for popsicles!" Zac and Ashley handed the ice cold treats to the exhausted players as they left the field. Little did we know, these were the boys who would renew the winning tradition for the Bearcats and greatly impact the future of our family. Those early memories are some of our favorites.

Whether in middle school, high school, college, or the professional ranks, coaches' wives across the United States speak the same language. It is comforting to be together. Our husbands' devotion to the profession of athletics has united us forever. Perhaps you are just beginning the adventure. Every coach's wife could write a book about her experiences. In order to let you know that you are not alone in your experience and to find out what coaches' wives *really* think, I surveyed over 400 coaches' wives. This book represents the combined wisdom of these tough and tender women who have weathered storms long enough to enjoy the resulting rainbows. I strove to use their words as much as possible. I hope you will see yourself in the hundreds of quotes throughout this "playbook."

What Were the Early Days Like?

Adjusting to Loneliness

As with anyone beginning a new adventure, the early days for a coaching couple are filled with promise, hope, and disappointment. Deborah Ford said she "knew" she would be the "perfect wife, mother, and coach's wife." Sounds familiar, doesn't it? However, being "perfect" doesn't keep him home. One wife explained, "As newlyweds, I would get my feelings hurt if he was gone a lot. I tried to be the perfect wife and cook and clean and keep a perfect house. My biggest pet peeve was to cook a 'good' dinner and not know what time he was going to come home—and more often that not when he did come home, he had already eaten."

After a few cold meals eaten alone, disappointment may set in. Fantasies of being the perfect wife to the perfect husband did not materialize. One wife explained that "I placed a lot of pressure on myself to always be positive and made sure that I never did anything that would reflect badly on Steve. During the last days of our honeymoon, Steve had his first job interview at Grapevine High School. Nervous about making a good impression, I answered almost all of Steve's questions for him. He was hired in spite of this. We both agreed that it would probably be best if he answered the questions from then on!"

Another wife was so overwhelmed by her new situation that

she felt "confused, lost, and did not know how to fit in." These feelings are common for people in new coaching situations.

Some women are simply uninformed about the amount of time a coaching husband must spend away from his family. "I had a difficult time in the beginning because I wasn't prepared for him to be away from home so much," began a young wife. "I grew up the daughter of a farmer and never wanted to marry one because they were always working. I didn't realize that when I fell in love with a coach that it would be the same way." Another wife was also taken by surprise. "We were both in college when we met, and he had just graduated when we married. I had no idea what being married to a coach would be like. We married August 16th, and the day we returned from our honeymoon was the start of two-a-days. He dropped me off at our new home (full of unopened boxes), and I didn't see him again for nine months. I wasn't very understanding, and we were pretty miserable for the first year. I thank God our marriage survived."

Others simply didn't want to believe it. Michelle Hugg said, "Before I got married, people tried to prepare me. They told me I would never see him during football months and when I did see him he would be too tired or too distracted to notice me. Of course, I didn't believe it, not really. My husband and I lived far apart for two years before we were married, so I felt that I was prepared for anything, even football season. Well, I was wrong. Those months were often very lonely especially because I was away from my family and friends for the first time. At times I felt that I had been deserted, left to handle everything alone. Sometimes I felt we had been cheated out of those "wonderful newly married months." At times I was resentful and angry. I would tell myself that it was not his fault and that he was only doing his job. I would try to be cheery and supportive. I wanted his home life to be a refuge, free of stress and thoughts of work. At times I succeeded, at times I failed miserably. At my worst I cried and yelled at my husband. I learned quickly that this behavior only makes us both feel horrible. I was the happiest when I made the most of that precious time I had with my husband and the time I had alone."

When we yell instead of listening (and we *all* do it), pout instead of support, blame instead of taking responsibility for our responses, and hold grudges instead of forgive, we become most angry with *ourselves*. And that is one kind of anger that our husbands can do nothing about.

Adjusting to poverty

The new wife of a coach knows that there are struggles ahead, and she believes that she can face them because her love is strong, but often love must be helped by determination. Melanie Simon's family faced financial difficulties early on. "The first two years were rough," she explained. "Four months after we were married, the UTEP football staff was fired, and Matt ended up taking a part-time assistant position at Washington. It was tough. We had to deplete his IRA just to eat and pay the rent. I can remember once there were ice cubes and hamburger buns in the freezer–nothing else." As told in *It's More Than Just A Game*, Ann Bowden remembers, "There were plenty of times that we couldn't afford to go places or do things. I remember how tight finances were when we lived in that old Army Air Corps barracks at South Georgia Junior College. I remember what it was like to raise six children on less than $5,000 a year." Sometimes a coaching couple's initial standard of living is far below what the wife experienced before she married, and she may be surprised at the resentment she feels because of this. However, if one responds properly, these struggles as well as others can powerfully bond a couple together.

Adjusting to New Expectations

Some of those early, embarrassing moments, when we just weren't sure what people expected of us, make wonderful stories later. Leslie Baca recalls, "I was very naive and impressionable. I remember Eddie was going over to a coach's house one evening for a special social time, and I went along, of course, to visit with the other wives, but I was the only one there! I asked the host where his wife was. He said she had gone to bed! I did not realize that wives were so often cut out of the picture." There Leslie was sitting in a room full of men–trying to smile. Katherine Wood explained that "perhaps the hardest part for me was 'growing up' into the role of being wife and a coach's wife." Learning how to mesh the "role" with your talents and preferences is, perhaps, a lifelong challenge, but one certainly worth taking!

In a Nutshell

Linda Griffin creatively sums up the experience of many new coaches' wives this way:

Being very young I was unaware of:

Cold Meals	Hot Tempers
Early Meetings	Late Hours
Up for Games	Down for Conversation
Loyal Wives	Disloyal Fans
Crowded Days	Lonely Nights
Happy Kids	Disgruntled Board Members
Soggy Shoes	Sunburned Heads
Long Meetings	Short Greetings
Exhilarating Fridays	Gloomy Saturdays
Tunnel Vision	Glorious Dreams
District Heroes	Bi-district Bums
Brilliant Winners	Lonely Losers

The Purpose of the Early Days

Few truly experience the purpose of the sorrows and joys *as* they happen; the experiences are just too strong emotionally. In sorrow, we often ask, "Why is this happening to me?" In joy, we sometimes say, "I don't know why this is happening, but I'll take it." The truth is that years may pass before a specific purpose may be revealed; however, the general purpose for the married couple is clear. The "early days" of a marriage are designed to cement a couple together. During courtship, you may have felt "velcroed" to your man. During engagement, you may have felt glued; however, neither velcro nor glue is strong enough to hold a marriage together. You need cement, and emotional cement is produced through the joys and challenges experienced in those first months and years of marriage.

If you are a newlywed, don't be fearful of this truth–just

realize its importance. You will fail. You will not be the perfect wife. He will not be the perfect husband, but that's okay because emotional cement requires failures as well as successes in the mix. Failure will not destroy a marriage. Refusing to learn from failure will.

The early days should also be a time when you create special memories. Later in life, during a quiet moment or even a tense moment, one of you may say, "Remember when we were first married and we..." or "I remember when the kids and I came to the gym one day and..." or "I'll never forget when you and the cheerleaders made that run-through sign that said..." After all, in the end, it's our memories that count.

Keys to Successful Early Years

The first and most important key I learned was to submit early. Now, don't close the book and throw it in the trash. Submission is actually just another word for "winning through compromise." I have rarely seen coaching couples who have succeeded when he had to compete both on the field (or court or track) and at home. Most wives resist "submitting" to their husband's leading, their husband's career, their husband's ideas because there is something that they want or need for themselves—control, love, attention, an independent identity—and they are afraid that they won't get it. Although it may sound strange, if you'll be patient, and read the rest of this book, you will see that by choosing to let your life be guided by *his* career and *his* plans, you will actually obtain more of what you want and need than you will by fighting his career choice or by trying to change him. Therefore, the earlier you agree to submit, the sooner you'll get more of what you need.

Second, the smartest and wisest wives realize that the best way to walk through life is to waste nothing and that includes struggles. By *leaning into* the struggle instead of *running away from* it, a young wife gains strength to face the next obstacle. Leaning into struggles involves looking for options instead of complaining and feeling helpless. If you don't see him as often as you would like, how can you make your presence known to him? Put a note in his wallet, place your "song" in the cassette player of his car, or make him a special breakfast. Leaning into means to be thankful for what you have and patient concerning what you don't have. A wise woman once said, "You *can* do anything you want to do. You just can't do it all right now."

Last, always remember that the "big picture" is quite different from what you may be experiencing at the moment. Today, you may be unhappy with a situation or disappointed in yourself, but it will not always be this way. There will be more fulfilling times ahead as long as you leave room for them. Some women fill their lives with so much resentment and bitterness that there is simply no room for happiness and joy to take root and grow. So, today he forgot your birthday or your anniversary. Today, he chose to stay an extra hour watching video replays instead of coming home to your warm meal. Learn from your pain and disappointment, and remember that the "big picture" involves more than what you feel right now.

TO THE GAME...

CHAPTER TWO

Realities—
The Life of a
Coach's Wife

Just think of all the hats a coach's wife can wear: wife, daughter, mother, grandmother, fan, friend, employee, boss, church member, neighbor, housekeeper, cook, cheerleader, taxi driver, hostess, "finder" of every hidden item(!)... No wonder we are so tired!

No matter where our husbands coach, even if it is in Little League, we share a sisterhood as coaches' wives. It is a treasure to value. Beautiful friendships develop because of our husband's career.

Fitting In

Perhaps the most awkward part of being a coach's wife is the time when you are new to a staff. You ask, "How do I fit in?" "Are there other wives on the staff like me?" We feel apprehensive. We hope to find acceptance and maybe a good friend. Often we gravitate to the wives with whom we share commonalities: our career, our children, our hobbies.

Sometimes you are part of a whole new staff; other times you are the only new person. It is especially nice to have another wife reach out to help you feel a part of the new "family." If that doesn't happen, it can feel lonely. But don't have a pity party! Pick up the phone and get acquainted with other wives. Ask questions about the new community. Take the initiative—invite another staff couple over. You may feel you have the smallest apartment or house, but remember we are all in the same business!

Getting Together

Usually the head coach's wife sets the tempo for participation in the season's activities. Our staff is large with 17 coaches and most wives are active. We start with a wives' salad supper in August to plan our after-game parties. One year, we had a slumber party at a hotel and Susan Keeling (former president of the American Football Coaches' Wives Association) gave a mini-seminar on being a coach's wife. She was inspirational, and it helped us all put on our "game face" for the season!

Two years ago, two assistants' wives, Lacretia Churchman and Elaine Brevard, hosted a Halloween costume party. We all know how reluctant coaches are to socialize during the season, but with other coaches they can really relax. The outfits were a riot! We then played a version of the "Newlywed Game." The Churchmans' home was comfortable, but not large; I write this to encourage assistants to have get-togethers at their homes. It promotes a family feeling and often relieves the head coach's wife of being the planner.

For party ideas, survival tips, laughs, and over 350 recipes, turn to "Winning Seasons," the 1996 cookbook of the American Football Coaches' Wives Association. Liz Mullins and Joyce-

Anne Hamlin have put together a winner! Contact AdCraft Associates at 7108 Fairway Drive, Palm Beach Gardens, Florida 33418, or call 561-625-1610 for your copy.

Expectations

Coaches' wives often wonder if there will be expectations on them. Ideally, there is an atmosphere of freedom where the wives can be themselves. Some like to be involved, while others value their privacy.

I grew up in San Antonio, and our moving to Ballinger (population 4,400) was an adjustment. I recall walking into the bank and grocery store and feeling the eyes follow me. People would whisper, "That's the new coach's wife." They then asked me questions about our home, church preference, etc. and at first I felt uneasy. When I realized they just wanted to know us, I relaxed. I politely declined invitations to join organizations and instead, carved my own niche. We had moved from a community that had a library "story hour" for preschoolers, so I offered to start one at their Carnegie library, and it was a hit! I wanted to live up to my *own* expectations, not someone else's.

Attendance

Going to your husband's games is really up to *you!* When our husbands played athletics, they loved to perform for friends and family in the grandstands. Now in their role as coach, they must stand on the sidelines and hope their detailed instruction and preparation will result in victory. Most coaches want their loved ones to share exciting moments. Most wives want to be near for that hug after a painful loss. Being there says, "I love you."

The logistics of going to the games isn't always easy. Part of the adventure may be getting off work, arranging child care, or packing the children. It is a rare luxury to live near grandparents who can babysit. And you have to prepare for all kinds of weather! At our home games, the staff families sit in a reserved section under the press box.

Attending the away games can mean driving across town or traveling all day. It is helpful if the wives form travel groups before the season starts. Our groups seem to form according to departure time and whether or not we take children. Feelings sometimes get hurt if we don't speak up. When you have a question about whom to ride with, call to ask for a ride, rather than feel left out. If you do have children, arrange for child care unless the driver asks you to bring them along.

Loyalty

Coaching is a people business. It is about giving, not getting. So the effort of building up each other demands loyalty: loyalty of the coach's wife to her husband, her husband's team, staff, administrators, etc. This is perhaps most important in a small community where the coach's wife is more visible. We have to be careful when we give our opinions in public because others may perceive what we say as speaking for our husbands. Be positive! This is not Pollyanna advice. Coaches leave a big impression on people, and no one forgets a coach. When you move on, the coach's wife may be forgotten, but it is remembered if she was a liability to him or an asset!

During a tense season (they all are!), you may need to vent to someone. It is not disloyal to talk openly to a trusted friend. Our staff wives had a Bible study twice a month for the first time this past season. Several wives came regularly, and it was helpful to talk about frustrations. We weren't there to solve each other's problems, but it was soothing to open our hearts to each other in a safe environment, and to look to God for help.

There will be times that our husbands are wrong. It is not disloyal to bring it to their attention, but we need to do so privately and lovingly. While it is difficult to find a good time for such a conversation, it is indeed being loyal to help him see blind spots.

Keeping Confidences

Husbands look to their wives for balance. So, naturally, at home he will "unload" events of the day. Coaches' wives will hear stories that need to be kept confidential. Be a good listener and hold back advice unless asked. Then tuck the "news" under your hat and bite your tongue when you'd like to add that "confidence" to a later conversation. Coaching husbands value the trust they can place in us.

Gossips love to hear the inside story, especially during the season. They want to know who is injured or why a player was sidelined for disciplinary action. For years, I was naive and did not realize that fans use this information to place bets on a game.

At home, Randy may mention details of a conversation with an administrator or player. If he was worried that I would tell these things to anyone else, he would guard his words. I don't seek to glean juicy details of his day, but I do want him to feel comfortable telling me what is on his heart.

Coaching Jobs

Coaching jobs aren't found in the classifieds. Mary Joseph reminds us that "young coaches learn about the profession and job openings by spending time with the respected veterans, going to clinics, and 'shooting the bull.'" A coach is hired based on reputation: playing experience, coaching record, his contributions on a successful staff, communication skills, physical appearance, morals and ethics, and family life. A breakdown in any one of these areas can be a liability to a coach. Can a coach's wife make a difference in her husband's career? A supportive coach's wife can enhance her husband's resume and reputation. As she is growing as a person and learning new skills, her enthusiasm for new ideas can help her husband. They may think of new fund raising ideas, work together with the Fellowship of Christian Athletes, or develop innovative ways to involve administrators and boosters.

I have often thought, "A wife will not cause her coach to win more games, but she *can* contribute to losses." A coach's wife is no different from any other wife; yet the pressures on her husband are so concentrated, intense, and public during the season that she must often hold up both ends of the relationship for several weeks. In every season the coach faces many distractions related to the team: illness, injuries, eligibility, travel problems, booster interference, media demands, the weather, and budget concerns. It requires a wife's unselfish love to carry the home front for those weeks. It is a wise husband who appreciates such a wife and credits her.

Support for the Coach's Wife

Sometimes, part of "fitting in" as a coach's wife is feeling understood. Having a network of friends, family, and other coaches' wives certainly helps.

There are two *free* newsletters published to help coaches' wives. The American Football Coaches' Wives Association publishes a quarterly one. The Fellowship of Christian Athletes publishes, "Behind the Bench." It's described in the last chapter. The addresses are listed in the bibliography. Get on the mailing list of both!

CHAPTER THREE

The Head Coach's Wife

What is it like to be a *Head* coach's wife?

> *Head tables
> *Head of the line
> *Headlines
> *Headaches!

It is an unpaid job, and it can be a joy or a burden. There are privileges and responsibilities.

Privileges

The visible perks of being a head coach are the higher salary, often a travel allowance, maybe a country club membership, and the "fame." Of course, that fame is very fragile! The head coach's wife gets to enjoy the benefits of her husband's position. She (unofficially) represents him in the community. It gives her a certain status and recognition, even an identity. There are sometimes travel opportunities to conventions and speaking engagements.

The greatest privilege, however, of being the wife of the

head coach is being a servant. Having walked in the shoes of the assistants' wives, she can empathize. She knows the demands, the patience, and the sacrifices that are being made in their homes. The staff wives may look to the one in front as having the "power" and "position," but the one in front is really a servant to those who look to her. It is an honor to be entrusted with that influence. It requires humility for success.

Mentoring

The head coach's wife has learned what it's like to be on the other side as an assistant and can be sensitive to their struggles. She can warmly welcome a new wife to the staff. Cindy Campbell said that when they joined the staff at University of North Carolina, Coach Dick and Shirley Crum sent her a dozen yellow roses. This thoughtful act made her feel immediately accepted.

My mentor was Bonnie Green in Bryan, Texas. When Randy and I moved from that staff to his first head coaching job, Bonnie surprised me with a mum corsage for our first game! Bonnie made me feel so good on that anxious day.

Often the head coach's wife does not realize her influence. Her experiences are valued by the younger wives. Donell Loyd and Lisa Coleman made a special effort to tell about their mentors in their responses to the questionnaire. Donell wrote about Mary Commalander and Marcy Foster. "Mrs. Commalander was a wonderful model for a new coach's wife. She was very calm, very organized and made everyone feel accepted. Mrs. Foster loved being a coach's wife and was very positive. We went to every practice!" Lisa Coleman added, "The first time I met

Delmarie Davis I knew she was special. She made every coach on her husband's staff and every wife feel like they were so important!" Certainly Donell and Lisa would have adjusted to their new schools well, but the head coaches' wives smoothed the way and taught them something in the process.

Not all head coaches' wives will feel obligated to fill such a role. Their personality may be more reserved. They may not be involved in their husband's career for many reasons. They may have their own career demands, illness, they may live outside the team's community or they may just be tired! A staff of enthusiastic wives can plan their own activities and invite the head coach's wife, who may or may not choose to participate.

Remembering what my mentor did for me, I decided to pass the gift along. In 1990 Kathy Harrell was moving to a remote town (population 3,000) for her husband's first head coaching job. I wrote her the following letter:

Jan. 8, 1990

Dear Kathy,

I am excited about the adventure ahead of you! I wanted to write down some things I remember about the "first coaching job" and maybe they will help you:

1. Seek things in the town you admire and appreciate and tell people that. Introduce yourself and remember names. (This will help Sam when you can help him.)

2. Don't jump to get involved in all the clubs that people want you to join (Beta Sigma Phi, Women's Club, etc.). I put them off by saying I needed to go through a season and have all my

attention for Randy and the kids to make the adjustment.

3. Get a babysitter (take the kids there) or Mother's Day Out once or twice a week and/or a night out to have a break. Randy had so much to do that I could easily feel sorry for myself carrying the load of "home." (Spend the day in a bigger city or go home and do something you want to.)

4. Realize that some of the people who are eager to meet you will expect you to meet their expectations and later, if you don't, they will turn on you. (Parents)

5. Beware of saying too much too soon—never tell anything Sam may tell you in confidence or about anyone he works with.

6. It will seem that everyone is related to each other!

7. Be ready to listen when Sam wants to unload or just talk. (Too often I want to give my expert opinion back.) You will be the only one he can be completely open with. It takes a long time to know who to trust and sometimes it's not anyone.

8. Be creative—try to think of ways he can keep his job fun (the cheerleader in you). Put signs around the house to build him up: Get your colors—Blue and Gold and mascot—Owls—things. Start your loyalty to your new school. I know the kids love that.

9. You won't live there forever, so don't put a lot of importance on things money can buy. You are so talented and cute and creative.

10. Accept the traditions and be tolerant of those which don't matter. Promote positive feelings about the program. Don't be

afraid to let people you meet know that Sam is a winner and you know he'll do a great job.

Kathy, these are random thoughts, but I hope they help you in the transition. You'll be a great head coach's wife!

Love,
Carolyn

Kathy recently asked me if I remembered writing that letter. She said it has meant so much to her. In fact, she keeps it tucked in her lingerie drawer. We never know how much our encouragement means to someone!

Responsibilities

The foremost responsibility has already been discussed: loyalty. It is not always easy. Sometimes we resent the demands on our husbands. We may resent that their value is unappreciated. The "high road" is to seek integrity and remain loyal to the whole system.

I have alluded to the role of hostess. This varies greatly according to the wife's personality and the staff's personality. Some staffs like to be socially active; others "do their own thing." When parties are planned, the head coach's wife welcomes initiative and help from the group. Often the most difficult hurdle is getting the word out. One thing is sure, "don't rely on the husbands to tell the wives!"

A responsibility that can be heavy is that of being alone. Kelly Smith's husband has been an assistant coach at Howard Payne, North Texas, SMU, Baylor, and Arkansas. He is now the head coach at a large Dallas high school. Kelly said, "I loved being one of the group. It is difficult to be a head coach's wife. It can be lonely. There are unique situations when you don't have anyone to confide in. The up side is that we see Scott a lot more now that he is coaching high school. He is home in the evenings; and we can spend Thanksgiving and Christmas at home. We used to always have the suitcase out."

Unless she has been in coaching, a mother or sister can't feel the heaviness that the head coach's wife feels. They can be wonderful support and friends, but the complete rapport is not there. That is why it is important to keep communication open with your husband, so he is aware of your needs and you can keep each other going through the season. The aloneness can actually draw your marriage closer together.

The head coach's wife feels the responsibility of keeping communication open with the staff wives. Donell Teaff (Baylor, American Football Coach's Association) knows the delicate art of balancing the relationships with the wives. "Be kind, keep in touch, but just as he (the head coach) has to keep some distance because of his role, so the wife has to maintain it." The head coach's wife is simply "one of the girls" when the wives get together. However, when the subject shifts to coaching business and the policies of her husband, the head coach's wife has to politely pull back. For example, a wife recently was telling me of their financial problems, and I was helping her with job options. She then said her husband's coaching assignment had been changed, and they were going to be making less money. That fell under Randy's business as the head coach, and I knew it was off limits for me to discuss.

The most challenging responsibility for the head coach's

wife is that of being the encourager. It is the role that hits highs and lows. Being a cheerleader is natural for many coaches' wives. And since opposites attract, the serious, focused coach needs her for balance! Being an encourager means being able to keep the big picture in mind. It means accepting that 80 percent of people will like you, and 20 percent will not, no matter what. Don't let the 20 percent depress you!

We are responsible to gracefully accept being under authority. Even though the head coach carries a position of authority, he always has to answer to higher authorities. He is a cog in a big machine, usually a school system. Therefore, he often needs our encouragement to keep a healthy perspective. Sometimes the school system has its own agenda for athletics, and the head coach has to battle on behalf of the assistants and players to protect and provide the best chance for success. The focus for a coach is the working out of dreams. The focus of administrators is the working out of budgets and images. These battles can be emotionally draining for the head coach. By keeping the big picture in mind, the head coach's wife can listen, understand, care for, and encourage her husband. She can lift herself and her husband above the circumstances so as to not take them personally, but it's not easy!

Other Roles to Learn From:

There are other wives with demanding roles and we can learn from them:

Doctor's wife, Laurie Harper, mother of four, says:

Doctors' wives learn to be very independent even to a fault. While it is true the demands on our husbands take them away from home, it is a mistake to begin to exclude them from being part of a family's routine. We try to wait dinner until he comes home because we know he is trying his best to get here on time. I depend upon his duties around the house because I have seen wives and families become so independent that they practically phase out his role. Many physicians then seek another place where they are needed.

Pastor's wife, Charlotte Bruster (Missouri, Arkansas, Oklahoma, Tennessee, Texas)

Ministers' families are often referred to as living in a fish bowl where every action is observed. I think the most important role for me as a minister's wife is to be myself, letting God work His plan for who I am. If I am content with myself I can help my family deal with the often-interrupted lifestyle of a minister's family. If we can see the overall picture of being and doing what God wants for us, whatever our vocation, we can deal so much more constructively with the disappointments and inconveniences that come our way.

Military wife, Frances "Sissy" Seyle (South Carolina, Texas, Nebraska, Alabama, Oklahoma, California, Louisiana, New York, New Hampshire)

"Flexibility is the key to Air Power." This is a common saying in the Air Force. And, flexibility is the key ingredient for the lifestyle of the military family as well. The constant moving requires you to keep your bags ready to pack most of the time. We are termed military dependents. However, in reality we have to be very independent to survive. You truly have to love the red, white and blue to accept such a nomadic lifestyle.

President's wife. Margaret Truman, daughter of President Harry Truman wrote about her mother in *First Ladies*:

A few days after the Trumans moved into the White House in 1945, my mother received one of the nicest letters of her life from Grace Coolidge. It was full of understanding and encouragement from someone who could really empathize with her situation.... It meant a lot to mother to know there was another woman out there who had been through it all and was rooting for her—even if she was a Republican.

In *First Ladies*, Margaret Truman also told of a compassionate letter Nancy Reagan received in 1981 from Jacqueline Kennedy Onassis after President Reagan was wounded by a would-be assassin.

Political differences and rivalries pale in the midst of real tragedy. If a "rival's" coach's wife is experiencing pain, send her a note to express your compassion. Your kindness will be especially appreciated.

A head coach's wife may live in a small community or be recognized by TV cameras, but in either case, eyes are upon her. She has a sphere of influence because of her husband's job. Coaches may not be in the business of making life and death decisions, but they are intimately tied to the dreams of many,

many people. The coach's wife shares in this intense behind-the-scenes pressure.

YOU MAY NOW KISS THE BRIDE, AND I WON'T CALL A HOLDING PENALTY.

CHAPTER FOUR

Marriage ·

"To have and to hold from this day forward, in sickness and in health, for better or worse, through wins and losses, as long as you both shall live."

Isn't that the vow we took?

Remember the affection with which he courted you? Men are natural conquerors, and *you* were the prize! He was so different then—he even enjoyed shopping together as a couple.

How do coaching marriages survive? My survey to 400 coaches' wives may not have been scientific, but it did reveal a lot of experience...1,526 total years of marriage! That is *teamwork*! Philda Dudgeon said, "I have more friends that have gone through divorces whose husbands are *not* coaches. Coaching seems to draw a family closer together, not push them apart."

Coach Ken Sparks

Of course there are some coaching marriages that do not make it. Coach Ken Sparks is the winner of four national championships at Carson-Newman College. He tells his own story hoping that other couples will avoid his mistakes:

It's not easy living with a coach. He is going 100 mph. He does it thinking that he is keeping you first. If asked, I would have said my priorities were God first, family second, and my job third, but that wasn't reflected in the way I spent my time. If I wasn't coaching 16 hours a day someone was going to get ahead of me. I was a good provider, protector, I was moral and I loved my family. But I had blind spots. My wife was not concerned with winning. Her needs were not being met. I was pushing myself so hard to be a good coach and was selfish. I wish she'd kicked me in the shin a few times before she said she didn't love me. The bitterness had built up. She didn't want to go places with me. We lived in two different worlds. I panicked and tried to fix it quick. But the wounds were there.

I was single for 11 years and raised two teenagers. I had to live with the scars of rejection, failure, and hurt. I came to rely on the peace I had in Christ. I told God, "I can't understand this, but I'll go where you want me to go in this." I never wanted to be humbled this way again. I had hope because of my hope in Christ. Because He is real. If He met me for salvation where I was at 18, He would be there for me again.

Coach Sparks is now remarried and devoted to his lovely wife Carol. Our son, Zac, plays football for Carson-Newman. Every February, Coach Sparks hosts a football clinic in scenic Gatlinburg, Tennessee. He encourages couples to attend for a romantic weekend in the Great Smoky Mountains. Randy and I have attended the past three years. While the men learn new football techniques, the wives are treated like royalty. Coach Sparks arranges first class speakers to help coaches' wives in their role. Randy and I agree that our marriage is better for our experiences there.

Now I understand that some of you reading this book did not marry a coach. You married a lawyer, a dentist, a salesman, a store manager, and you were prepared to support your husband in that profession, and then swoosh! Suddenly you're "the coach's wife" who must smile when she doesn't feel like it and share her husband with hundreds of strangers who feel as though they have the right to publicly criticize him. When you said "I do," you certainly were not aware of these specific challenges that lay ahead; however, you did not make a commitment to coaching, you made a commitment to a man who has chosen to be a coach. That is the foundation of understanding in the rest of this chapter. You do not have to feel "called" to be a coach's wife. You have already *chosen* to be his wife. In order to make the role easier, I and most of the women surveyed feel that the following concepts are important.

Understand the Time Commitment

As mentioned previously, the No. 1 complaint from coach's wives is the inordinant amount of time he must spend away from home. The first thing you must realize is that you will never be able to change this fact. The wives stressed repeatedly that "getting a grip" on your attitude concerning his time away is crucial. It just goes with the territory, and he cannot change it anymore than a doctor can walk away from an emergency. The profession demands that he practice, scout, or plan, and most of that must be done away from home. However, one wife shared the key to the struggle: "The less I demand or expect from him time-wise, the more he seems to call from the office or attempt to get us time together." That's it. The less we complain, the more they want to see us. I know that there are always exceptions. Sometimes we *must* ask for more of his time, but generally, especially during his season, the wife must make the best of the time she gets.

Remember this rule: *If you want to win, give in.* I know it sounds strange, but you'll never change the situation by complaining. Listen to the wisdom from these wives:

- (married 13 years) Realize things will pass. The seriousness and intensity of the season, or recruiting, or even during the first year in a new place will pass. There will be more relaxed times.

- (married 25 years) I see very few successful coaches with selfish wives.

- (married 21 years) I always find a good book to read during the season. I can escape from the pressure and not resent the time he spends watching video.

- (married 35 years) Never jump to conclusions when they are late. Learn to hold your tongue. Be flexible. Be willing to give–sacrifice pays great dividends. And never move or throw away a piece of paper with strange "doodlings" on it. It might be the winning plan.

Your winning plan must include a choice to *lean into* this part of coaching by refusing to complain. If he knows that a smiling face awaits him at home, he'll be cussing red lights to get there.

Increase the Communication

Most women agree that their No. 1 need is verbal communication. The truth is that most of us talk because we simply enjoy it. When a friend calls and says, "Hey, let's do lunch tomorrow," we look forward to a time of fun and friendship. When a friend calls your husband with the same proposition, he hangs up and says, "Hmm, I wonder what he wants." Strange isn't it. Men view conversation as a method of dispensing information. Women view it as recreation. More than one husband has said to his wife, "Would you get to the point!" And he's not making a request—it's a demand. Most men just don't understand the purpose of all those **words**. In fact, most women drown their husbands in words. Have you ever been in the middle of what you thought was an excellent story, and suddenly you realize that your husband's eyes are glazed over? He is nodding in all of the right places, but you know that he's not with you at all. The result of this situation is, at the least frustrating, and at the most, wounding. In a few homes, the typical "male" and "female" styles are reversed, and it's the husband who loves to talk while the wife likes the more condensed communication. However, most women spend their lives trying to get their husbands to talk more.

The ideal way to communicate is for *both spouses* to understand the needs of the other. However, in reality we can only change *our* behavior. Therefore, the following suggestions are for wives only.

1. You have a strong need for conversation. You cannot change that, and if your spouse cannot provide it, then find some friends

who can. Make regular dates and talk to your heart's delight. However, be careful not to make these times only "gripe" sessions. Venting is important, but complaining steals our emotional energy while laughing strengthens us.

2. You cannot change his need for more concise communication. Studies which compare the conversation styles of toddlers indicate that how much we communicate verbally is linked to genetics. Even at three years old, little boys just don't make as many verbalizations as little girls. They can't change it; you can't change it, but you can learn how to work with it.

For example, women love to tell stories from the beginning to the end, including all of the details and stretching out the suspense because we enjoy watching the reactions of the person listening. Randy calls this, "spinning a web." Men want it just the other way around (unless it's a football or fishing story, you understand). They like the bottom line first. Then they want just the highlights. For example, at dinner a wife may say, "I have to tell you what frightening thing happened today," and she begins the story with "I got up this morning and saw it was a beautiful day." Five minutes later, she is just at noon. "I watched CNN and they had this report about seat belts ..." By now, the husband is lost and frustrated. "What happened?" he may scream. Then the wife says with a pout, "Well, I was trying to tell you, but if you're going to rush me like that, I don't think I'll finish."

The wife could get much further if she had simply said between bites, "I almost had a wreck today." If she offers no more information, her husband will soon say, "Really, where?" "Oh, over by the University. You know that corner with the red light that's always out of order. I'm glad the kid on the bike wasn't hurt." Then, he'll drop his fork and say, "Okay, tell me the whole story." Now that you have hooked him, you must know that he doesn't mean "tell me the whole story." He means "tell me the facts about the wreck." But isn't that nicer to hear than "get to the point"?

3. Limit the number of stressful topics to be discussed—especially during his season. Pick your battles carefully. If you would like him to do ten things, pick three. You know your husband best. He might want the information written down on a list; he might find that insulting. Whatever you choose to do, do not go on and on about why you need it done. Often wives feel guilty about asking for help from their husbands, so they spend too much time explaining why they need something. If he wants to know why you're asking, he will usually ask. If he doesn't ask, he probably doesn't want to know, so don't explain.

The wives surveyed offered this practical advice concerning communication:

- Always make time to go on a date even if it is just walking or biking.

- Use humor.

- Remember to look into each other's eyes.

- Pray. God will send blessings to us in many forms; a good book, a new insight, more patience.

- Send special notes in his lunch.

- Keep it honest. Our motto: "If you don't want my spouse to know—don't tell me."

- Agree to sometimes disagree. Learn to compromise.

Communication between two people is as individual as kissing. Only you know what works in your relationship.

Work as a Team

If your special coach could handle his work alone, he wouldn't have married you. Therefore, "teamwork" (a word he understands fully), requires serious involvement on your part, but the women surveyed also seemed to agree that getting involved is what makes being a coach's wife fun.

- If you can afford it, eat out, hire someone to clean the house, and *go to the game.*

- Be best friends, not competitors.

- The family must love coaching and sports as much as the coach.

Gary Smalley and John Trent have a unique perspective concerning involvement in their book *The Blessing.* They explain that, if you want to make a person (especially a man) feel valued, then learn the vocabulary of his vocation. Several of the wives surveyed agreed, and one wife stated clearly: "Learn the rules, strategies, etc. of every sport he coaches, and be at the games. Even when our husbands are home, they're thinking about coaching. Chances are, if you don't know enough about what he's doing or if you haven't seen the game he's thinking of, your topics for discussion will be greatly reduced. Coaching is all-consuming, and your husband needs to be assured that you value what he does. We show this by being "informed, involved, and present!"

As I was writing this chapter, Zac and his bride of three weeks called from Tennessee. Jennie was asking me for a recipe, when she turned to Zac and said, "Are you going to watch that highlight video *again*?" She then asked me, "Is this normal? He watches the same football videos over and over." I laughed and said, "Yes, the apple doesn't fall far from the tree." Jennie was a Razorback cheerleader, so I knew she would like football. I'm not sure if she knew she would have to like it this much!

You may be a wife who truly *does not love* sports. However, by learning the vocabulary and rules and by learning about the players—their personal struggles and triumphs—you'll naturally become drawn to what your husband loves.

Being valued and respected is you husband's No. 1 need, and there is no greater way of expressing how much you value him than valuing what he does.

Build Your Relationship

Wouldn't it be nice if we could put "create a deep, intimate relationship with my husband" on our "things to do" list? We could work at doing it, get it just right, then scratch it off because once it's done, it should stay done. But, just like washing clothes and dishes, maintaining a good relationship is never truly "done." The wives surveyed overwhelmingly agreed that *commitment* is the true foundation for building and maintaining a lasting relationship. Here's another rule: *Anything worthwhile is inconvenient.* I could probably add that the more inconvenient something is the more worthwhile it is.

Being involved in your husband's coaching career and working around his schedule is inconvenient, but an overwhelming number of wives told me that it is certainly worth it. One wife of 32 years said it this way: "When you give love, you get love. Honor him and he will honor you. Stand by him always, and he will want you there. Always think about the good times in your marriage even though that is not always easy. Kiss him goodbye every time he walks out the door."

The wives in the survey also emphasized the need for spiritual strength and unity to maintain what their commitment started. These wives speak for many others:

- Be an encourager. Love the Lord and pray every day for your family.

- Stop looking at what you can get out of the relationship. If a relationship is built around giving, the rewards are immense. Share in the Lord's promise and love.

- The only secret for success in any marriage is the closer walk with the Lord regardless of the profession. (This wife has been married for 34 years.)

If you feel something is missing from your marriage, it could be this spiritual dimension. Search your heart and be open to the Lord to make your marriage stronger with His help.

Keep the Home Fires Burning

Your anniversary is a perfect time to renew your dreams together. Don't let the date sneak up on you. Anticipate it and make it special. Talk, plan, and budget for it. Brainstorm the possibilities: a hike, a train ride, reading poetry or selected passages to each other, attending a play, concert, or sporting events. You could go on a picnic, dine at home by candlelight or at a favorite restaurant. Your anniversary deserves special attention. A marriage is a living thing. Nurture it; reaffirm your love!

Attend to Unspoken Needs

Steve and Arlene De Bardelaben (Coral Gables, Florida) conduct marriage seminars that target college and professional coaches and athletes. They recently spoke at the annual Carson-Newman Clinic in Gatlinburg, Tennessee. They helped the couples to understand each other's needs and highlighted needs that require extra attention. Sexual needs is a topic which the coaches' wives survey did not address, yet Arlene wished it had been included. The bibliography includes ordering information for the following material they suggested: "Sex in a Growing Marriage" (a single audio cassette), by Ray and Anne Ortlund; *Love Busters,* and *His Needs, Her Needs* by Willard F. Harley, Jr.; and *Staying Close* by Dennis Rainey.

I purchased the tape first. It is short, sensitive, yet informative. As a biology major, I was not lacking in the fundamentals;

but like all of us, I was in a rut. It was time to be creative. The next week, Randy and I were traveling and decided to rent some books on tape. He picked out *Mars and Venus in the Bedroom*, by John Gray. We laughed and I was curious what it would be like to listen to it together. The information was terrific. There were times I felt a little embarrassed, which seemed ridiculous since we have been married for 21 years! After the tape was over, I said, "That was really good. I'm glad you picked it out for us." Randy replied, "Yeah, I liked it too the first time I listened to it." He had rented it before and just wanted me to hear it. That should tell us that husbands really *do* want us to be more aggressive and interested in their sexual needs.

Check It Out

Doris Wild Helmering (St. Louis Post-Dispatch) put together a marriage checklist that I found refreshing and practical. Most people who are married want to stay married. At the same time many spouses have behaviors that work against staying married. Are you or your mate guilty of any of the following?

Check those items that apply.

___Not talking. If you don't initiate conversations with your mate other than about the children or scheduling, how can your marriage be interesting?

___Talking too much. Chattering on endlessly about what you had to eat or drink, your golf game, and who said what does not invite your mate to listen to you. Instead, it invites him to tune out and head for the outdoors, away from you.

___Getting too angry. If you get angry at the drop of a hat, you're definitely inviting your mate to put up some insulation. Why? Because she's never sure when you'll hit her with a barrage of hostility.

___Breaking promises. It's hard for your mate to trust you or feel close and loving when you keep pulling the rug out from under her.

___ Not making a decision. Causing someone to wait, and wait, may be your way to stay in control. But it's also a way to convey that you don't care enough about your mate and his discomfort to make a decision.

___ Bringing nothing to the table. Most of us want an interesting partner who has a life outside of housework and watching television. When was the last time you read an article or attended a class or lecture and discussed it with your partner?

___Having a poor appearance. You might not think it matters how you look after 23 years of marriage, but your partner cares if you're overweight, frumpy or ill groomed.

___Constantly criticizing. One critical comment per week may not destroy closeness. But a continual barrage of criticisms about your mate's bad behaviors will. How many critical comments did you level in the last three days?

___Not making friends. As a couple you may feel little need for friends. At the same time, having friends brings energy and laughter and new ideas to a marriage.

___Showing no interest in sex. If you don't approach your mate, or don't respond when your mate approaches you, you're inviting trouble. Your mate may not seek an affair, but the opposite sex can certainly look more interesting.

___Pouting. When you get your feelings hurt, you may have learned to go underground and stop talking. More than three hours of refusing to talk erodes any marriage. It completely cuts off the conversational blood flow.

___Refusing to share chores. Being too responsible will invite your mate to take you for granted and cause your resentments to build. Not pulling your weight will invite your partner to become critical and cause you to feel resentful.

___Drinking too much. When you have too much to drink you are not available entirely. Your drinking also results in other behavior such as withdrawing, being aggressive, non-communicative, and overspending.

Take stock. As I said before, most people want to stay married, but they work against themselves with bad behaviors. Do you see yourself in this list?

Don't Marry A Coach

Wives tend to agree that being married to a coach requires maturity and unselfishness. In fact, before one says "I do" to a coach, she might want to read the poem Jackie Sherwood submitted:

Don't Marry A Coach

Don't marry a coach
Unless you can conceal your pain or
sit in the rain
at a football game.

Don't marry a coach
Unless you can cry at day
and at night act gay
while he has HIS say.

Don't marry a coach
Unless you can hold your tongue
When the phone has rung
and someone says "Your FLING
has been FLUNG."

Don't marry a coach
if disappointment you can't take
or bear to see his heart ache
'til it nearly does break.

Don't marry a coach
Unless you can realize
when THAT BIG JOB doesn't materialize
that grass just LOOKS greener
on the other side.

Don't marry a coach
if you can't move out in a hurry
when things go topsy-turvy
and you get thrown a curvy.

Don't marry a coach
UNLESS YOU LOVE HIM, I guess
So I'll really have to confess
that coaching IS an enjoyable mess.

Author unknown

COACH'S KIDS

CHAPTER FIVE

Family Life

Beverly Harkness remembers the September night their first son was born: "How dare my doctor induce labor on a Friday night! Keith took his game clothes to the hospital. It was his first year as the defensive coordinator for the Killeen Kangaroos! But by 5:30 P.M. there was no baby. The doctor announced that he *also* had to be at a game, so he was going to do a C-section. Our nine-pound son was born an hour later! I was glad Keith decided to stay. The Killeen Kangaroos won the state championship that year!" Beverly knew that her baby was learning the basics of living in a coaching family from the beginning—life revolves around the game.

Although the coaching family is, in many respects, just like any other family, it possesses unique characteristics that create both challenge and fun. For example, one wife stated, "My son says we have four seasons: football, hunting, track, and summer!" Only someone from a coaching family fully understands that statement. Our world centers around sporting events. Some wives state that they "don't have much of a family life," and many others said that they are basically "on their own" during their husband's season; however, the wise mother simply turns games and scouting trips into family time. Several women mentioned that even practice becomes a family time as their children grow familiar with the players and rules. It's another way of surrendering to the situation in order to obtain more of what you want.

One wife describes her circumstance: "From August through November I feel our family consists of me and the kids, which is hard; however, there are some great advantages to this occupation. The boys get to really be a part of Sam's job. They get to know the players, ride the bus, and experience the 'excitement of Friday night.' They understand what their dad does. My oldest son even told me once that he thought his dad being a coach made him more popular. When the season is over I really appreciate having Sam home and doing things as a family with both Mom and Dad. I'm sure I would take this for granted if I didn't go through those few months every year without him."

Although they don't often express it, coaching fathers and husbands often feel torn during their season because they know they often fail to meet their family's needs. Ken Berger from the Associated Press wrote a wonderful article on coaches who find that they spend more time with other people's kids than with their own. Jim Mora of the New Orleans Saints said, "I've never neglected my job for my family, but I have neglected my family for my job. I don't know many coaches who haven't." This truth is painful, and many men do not like having to make these choices. As coaches, they want to succeed, and they know the cost in time and energy that must be paid to obtain that prize; however, they want to succeed at home as well. Wise wives help husbands figure out ways to do both. For example, Marty Schottenheimer of the Kansas City Chiefs flew through a snowstorm on a private plane to watch his son play in a state football championship and immediately flew back to board the team plane for the Chiefs' game. He said, "If I had it to do over again, I'd do exactly what I did. I don't care who you are, where you start, or where you finish, the only thing that matters in this life is your family."

Being a coach's child has special benefits as well. One wife explained, "When your babies are born healthy, all is right with the world! Flowers arrived in a sports motif container with school-color ribbons. Instantly, the girls are Daddy's cheerleaders and the boys are assigned a position on the team! They grow up at the field or in the gym." From the beginning, they are exposed to competition. They witness first hand the benefits of courage, the power of endurance, and the advantages of self-control.

Most coaches' kids value being close to the action. For example, sons can be a part of the "inner circle." They can attend team meetings, ride the bus, or be in the locker room. They have an intimate view of their father in the heat of the battle. This experience is magnified if the son plays for his dad. In our family, Zac played quarterback for his father at his father's alma mater. The bond was tight during those four years.

Experiences for girls are unique as well–just ask our daughter, Ashley. She was a 1996 Homecoming Queen nominee. She and the other girls in the Queen's Court circled the field in convertibles, waving at the crowd, smiling, waving, smiling, waving. We had done everything possible to make this the perfect evening for her–hair, dress, shoes, make-up. However, when she stepped out of the convertible, her father was nowhere in sight. Her face reddened. Where could he be? Suddenly, Randy burst out of the dressing room and sprinted 100 yards in front of the crowd to proudly escort her to the middle of the field. Yes, indeed, he created a memory–one that only a coach's daughter could have! Yes, we have it on video tape.

Amanda McQueen, a high school senior, describes another feature of being "the coach's daughter." "You aren't dateless and pathetically bored because you're too tall, too short, too shy, and have the wrong hair color, or because of the zit you have hidden under your bangs; it's because every boy, not only in the high school but in the entire district, cowers under a rock at the mention of your father's name. And no matter how tough he was on Friday night, he can't find the courage to ring your doorbell on Saturday night." Most coaches like it this way, but their daughters sometimes wish they could change their names!

The following letter from Tracy Teaff seems to sum up the benefits and frustrations of being a coach's daughter.

My father has always been a football coach and last year he retired from coaching to become the Executive Director of the American Football Coaches Association.

I am 34 seasons old, having aged in seasons rather than years. Football games, recruiting, spring training, and two-a-days were my fall, winter, spring, and summer. As a young girl, footballs replaced dolls. I watched games instead of cartoons, wrote reports about sports, watched everything from Pee-Wee to Canadian ball, read the sports page instead of books, and watched reruns of games when the season was over.

Because of the pride I had in my dad, Baylor, and the running of the program, I had no trouble learning to stand up for what I believed in or to hold my head high and be proud of who I was.

The principles I learned from my father are the same I

learned from him at home. I continue to incorporate them into my life. Although coaching revolves around winning and losing, I was fortunate enough to experience it where the ultimate goal was not winning, but rather how you play the game.

What's it like growing up as a coach's daughter? It was like nothing else in the world. I have only one regret: I never got to play quarterback for my dad.

Tracy's letter corresponds with what many of the other respondents said: children benefit from being in a coaching family. Several mothers, however, warned that "some children choose a different path" besides athletics. Parents need to "allow the child space to have his own identity" and be aware of their own biases.

I will always be glad our children pursued their musical interests by singing in choir and in their senior musicals, "Oklahoma!" and "The Sound of Music." The friendships and confidence gained rounded out their personalities, so that sports wasn't their only school activity. After Ashley and Randy sang a duet in a school concert (their Mother's Day gift to me), we received many favorable comments. It surprised people to see another side of them.

Even when children choose to participate in athletics, they may feel pressure to be the best player or to play Dad's old position. Common sense tells any parent that pressuring a child in this way will backfire; yet if we are not careful, we'll do it anyway. Being objective is impossible. My best advice is to find some friends who have both common sense and honesty; then give them permission to confront you at any time they see you putting undue pressure on yourself, on your husband, or your children. I learned a long time ago that the best friends I have are the ones who love me enough to risk making me angry.

Remember, while athletes strive to be All-American and receive glories from the media, it is the lasting relationships which become the most valuable trophy. If we can keep that in focus, we won't be so anxious for our children to be heroes. If we can raise children who know how to build each other up, they will develop the greatness that comes from humility and leadership.

Maintaining a healthy coaching family is not easy, but many respondents to the survey believe that the struggles produce strength. One wife actually said, "I wouldn't trade a day." Don't be surprised if your children create a family tradition out of coaching.

Ideas to Increase Family Time

"Noting" Family Time

A practical and inspiring book to encourage building family relationships is called, *Put Your Heart on Paper,* by Harriette Anne Klauser. She tells how others have used the written word to "stay connected in a loose-ends world." Her wonderful ideas motivate you to do the same for your family.

One technique that affirms relationships is to pass on compliments you hear about a family member in the form of a note. Often we hear good things and forget to pass them on. Klauser says to write down the compliment like a quote with a source. She says "Consider yourself a letter carrier. It is your job, come hail or sleet or snow, to forward any compliment you hear to the right address."

Tag-Team Praise

Another fun idea I call Tag-team Praise. The basic idea behind this activity is to give each family member a turn at being the focus of everyone's attention. This may be especially helpful during Dad's season when he may leave before children are up and come home after they are asleep. Here are the steps:

1. Obtain butcher paper (or wide colored paper) and drape a door with it. The front door is often the best place, but it is not necessary. However, be sure to choose a door that family members often pass by.

2. Attach the paper to the door and write a family member's name on top. When children are under 14, a family member should be the focus for only one week. If they are over 14, extend the time, but to no more than one month.

3. During the week (or month), every family member writes something positive about that person on the door. It's best if you don't make too many "rules" about this activity. It's not necessarily helpful to say, "Everyone must write at least one thing a day." This undermines the sincerity of the compliments. It is best to just set the example yourself. Any time you think of something positive about who that person is or what that person has done, go write it on the paper. Try to be specific. Saying, "You are nice" is not as powerful as saying "I appreciate the way you

helped the visitor in your Sunday School class find her way to the auditorium yesterday." Instead of saying, "You are helpful around the house," say "Thank you for making my bed this morning when I was running late." During the week, cards and handmade gifts may appear on the door. If you have very young children who cannot write, be available to scribe for them. Let them tell you what to say, and you write it down word for word, signing their name. Toddlers may want to draw *special* pictures as a gift to the one they love.

4. When the time is up, give the butcher paper to the person whose name is on it. It is their choice as to what to do with it. Some throw theirs away; some keep them forever.

The wonderful thing about Tag-team Praise is that everyone including Mom and Dad get a turn at being on the door. Busy fathers and mothers are also able to write their notes to children who can read them over and over as a reminder that, although Dad may not physically be here, he is still thinking of them.

Lifemapping

Our husbands are always setting team goals, so why not set goals for your family? Psychologist John Trent gave the term "lifemapping" to a technique I've used before. First, write down all the major events of your life on a time line (your birth, perhaps baptism, first job, graduation, college, marriage, births of children, moves, etc.) Now extend it to the future. Write in how old your children will be and your goals for them. This is something you and your husband may dream about. You can include the whole family in the planning.

One goal Randy and I shared for our children was for them to attend a Christian sports camp called Kanakuk-Kanakamo in Branson, Missouri. Randy and I had met there as counselors, so we knew its value first hand. We wanted Zac and Ashley to mature as Christ did: in wisdom, in stature, and in favor with God and man (Luke 2:52). This is the "Four-Square Life" taught at Kamp. We saved and planned our summers around Kamp when the children turned 10 and 12. Looking back now on their nine summers, they gained confidence and independence through making new friends, identifying role models, and learning to be responsible without parents. It has helped them make transitions smoothly.

A surprise blessing from Kamp: Zac met Jennie there! Ashley is currently at Baylor University, because of the tremendous influence of Christian Kamp counselors. And now she is working there as a Kamp counselor.

We want our children to benefit by being coaches' kids, but we want to equip them for finding their own identity. Lifemapping shows us where we've been and where we are going. If your goal is to keep your family strong, start dreaming on paper.

Family Vacations

Getting out of town in the off season is limited, so we have to make the most of our vacations!

The perfect age to take driving vacations is when your children are ages 8-12. After that they want to be with their friends on holidays, and some are beginning to be committed to sports' schedules. Now, where can a coaching family go that will keep

"Dad" happy? How about visiting college spring trainings? Our family did this for four years and they provided some of our favorite memories. We had eight days and limited money. First, we let Randy pick the school(s) and he checked to be sure it was in session during our break. Then we planned our trip.

1) Notre Dame, Purdue, Graceland
2) Arizona, Arizona State, USC, UCLA, Grand Canyon
3) Florida, Florida State, Miami, Disney World
4) USAF Academy, Colorado, BYU, skiing in Utah

We lodged on campus when available, or in KOA cabins or with friends and family along the way. Our souvenirs were T-shirts and spiral notebooks from the campus bookstores!

It's Worth It!

A family centered around Dad's coaching compromises many things in terms of calendar demands, privacy, financial prosperity, etc. But *togetherness* is a worthwhile and achievable goal. Coaching families can adopt our school's athletic slogan, "When you play one of us, you play all of us!"

CHAPTER SIX

Career

How fortunate we are as women to live in a day when we have so many opportunities open to us, so many careers to choose from! When I met Randy, I was a pre-med student at Texas A&M. He was already coaching. As soon as we became engaged, I redirected my career path to teaching. Being first in my family to go to college, I promised my parents that I would graduate. Three years later, I had my degree, a husband, and two children! I was so blessed and happy with my young family that it was an easy choice to sacrifice "things" for time with those I loved. Being a homemaker was fulfilling for me. As Zac and Ashley were in middle school, I began to substitute teach. When they approached graduation age, I decided it was time to think about my personal goals. My favorite volunteer positions utilized my skills with people, organization, publicity, and knowledge on health-related issues. I began to pray for a job that I would enjoy. After researching and asking a lot of questions, I found out that our school district was starting an employee wellness program. They had the exercise physiologist ready to begin and were just looking for an assistant. Wow! Three years later I am still amazed at how the Lord opened this door for me.

Perhaps my message to you is to understand the stages in

your life. There will be years that you can take classes, nurture your career, attend to your family, and hopefully retire! The order may be different for some of us, but if we are patient, we can be fulfilled.

Why Coaching?

When most wives explain why their husbands coach, they almost always use the word "calling." They say, "God has called him to be a coach" or "Coaching is his calling." What they mean is that there is a sense of destiny about this particular career choice. Those who love it feel as though they are uniquely fitted for this kind of work. Their talents, temperament, and experience equip them for working with students and parents, and their competitive spirit motivates them even through the tough times. Although there are frustrations and sometimes tremendous stressors, the coach who loves his job often has an unexplainable sense of serenity and joy because he believes that he is fulfilling the role in life that he was meant to fulfill. The wife who unwisely demands that her husband give up his fulfillment in order to provide her with a more "normal" way of life risks gaining in return a husband who is restless and resentful.

Finding Compatible Careers

I know that you will not be surprised at the career choices made by the wives who participated in my survey.

40% were teachers
20% were homemakers

20% were business professionals
16% were school related professionals
4% were full time university students

Clearly, most wives gravitate toward jobs that have two qualities: a compatible working calendar and mobility. The 20 percent who are business professionals sometimes experience conflict with time off and matching holidays. However, the other 80 percent are usually free when their husbands are. Therefore, most respondents expressed little or no frustration with meshing their husband's career with the job for which they get paid.

Mobility is the other important factor in the career chosen by these wives. You know that it is the rare coach who stays in one place for even five years especially in the beginning of his career; therefore, wives actually find more security in choosing careers that allow them to transfer jobs and job skills more easily. Moving is never simple, but having a job that is more easily transplanted from one place to another does alleviate some pressure.

Even the wives who have careers in the business world emphasize the importance of supporting their coaches. An advertising art director said, "Our vocations are worlds apart which makes each of our careers that much more special. I love what he does, and I am committed to supporting him likewise." A physical therapist said, "We are both interested in assisting people in setting their goals and helping others to keep in good physical condition." I'd also say that this coach made a good decision in choosing a physical therapist for a wife. If he strains a muscle, she treats him for free! Even though these careers are so diverse from coaching, the wives clearly consider what they do to be a partnership with their husband.

Although coaches' wives are employed in various ways, we are all juggling masters. Daily we do our best to keep all of the balls up in the air so that our lives are as tranquil and orderly as possible. Sure, we drop something occasionally, but if women competed for trophies in "creative life-management," coaches' wives would win every year at both the state and national levels. Some of you would even make the All-American team!

The Struggling Wife

Not everyone has resolved the conflict of whose occupation should be considered more important. There may be some newly married women and even some veteran coaches' wives who are struggling because they believe it is unfair for their husband's career to take precedence over their own. The truth is that most of us have struggled to some degree with this same idea. Even if we do not set our hearts on keeping a particular job or "moving up the ladder" in a specific career, there is still a certain level of resentment to be acknowledged and dealt with concerning career choices and career moves.

I think the first reason we struggle involves the issue of control. No one likes to be controlled. Anyone who has been around children (or husbands!) knows that. Given the choice between A and B, I might choose A, but if you tell me that I must choose A, then B suddenly becomes quite attractive. Most coaches simply take for granted that their wives will be willing to uproot themselves and their children in order to make a better career move. Often they don't ask; they just assume. When this happens, wives struggle because they feel they were not given a choice.

Some women also have difficulty allowing their husband's career to take precedence just because it seems so old-fashioned. Few women in the '90's publicly state that they believe happiness is found in making their goals compatible with and/or subservient to their husband's goals. "Come on!" many women say. "That idea went out with Mrs. Cunningham on *Happy Days.*" However, my experience and the experience of the respondents clearly uphold the old-fashioned idea that a family is more unified when it is focused in one direction. Perhaps couples involved in other vocations have a different experience, but happy wives of successful coaches agree that all members of the family need to be playing on the same team, working together toward the same goal.

Another reason why we balk is because we honestly may not feel fulfilled. Somehow we feel that there are God-given gifts that we are not using. My challenge to you, then, is to learn more about your talents. Explore their many facets, then look for ways to use them that will be compatible with your husband's career. High school teacher Suzanne Starr has managed to follow her husband, Rob, through his professional football career, coaching, and school administration, while teaching math and raising a family. She learned to blend her artistic talent for color and design by mastering calligraphy, and working as a buyer for her mother's dress store. She didn't do it all at once; each had its own season.

PPQ

Judy Gregory, a coach's wife from West Point Military

Academy, conducted a workshop called "Working Wonders" at the American Football Coaches' Wives Association's convention. There, some coaches' wives expressed the frustration of their jobs taking a back seat to their husband's career choices. To help a coach's wife to find her niche, Judy suggested the "PPQ" method.

> **P** - stay **positive** about our husband's career even though it takes the family through separation, losses, and moves.
>
> **P** - **prioritize** by chopping overwhelming tasks into small pieces and doing the most important ones first.
>
> **Q** - **quality**. Remember that good relationships count more than anything else.

I hope these insights give you permission to "color outside the lines" a little, and gain a new perspective. We don't have to feel boxed in by our husband's career. No matter what Randy does for a living, I know that God is protecting and providing for me through him. It is ultimately God who is directing my life through moves, circumstances, and people. Resisting is not consistent with trusting the Lord. I choose to believe God's Word when He says, "For I know the plans I have for you, plans for your welfare and not for evil, to give you a future and a hope." (Jeremiah 29:11). And, "Trust in the Lord with all your heart, and lean not on your own understanding. In all your ways acknowledge Him, and He will make your paths straight" (Proverbs 3:5,6).

CHAPTER SEVEN

Getting Along

Coaching is a PEOPLE business! The coach and coach's wife have many professional relationships–staff, players, administrators, fans, etc., and many relationships become lifelong friendships! Maintaining protocol and enjoying the variety of people is another important item we must balance in our juggling routine. Coaches look to their wives to help them with remembering names, being active in the community, expressing gratitude, and attending functions.

Remembering Names

It is wonderful to call people, even those we rarely see, by name, but this skill can be nearly impossible for your husband to master. How many times at a banquet has he whispered, "What is Jim's wife's name?" and "What is Mrs. Rhiddlehoover's first name?" Coaches' wives have to be a walking rolodex! Maybe all the X's and O's and watching video numbs their brain for names.

I do try to keep names and faces matched correctly in my head, but Randy has taught me the *value* of this skill over the years. Twice when Randy began into new coaching jobs, he had pictures taken of the players and learned their names before arriving. We would go through the photos like flash cards until we both felt comfortable matching names and faces. It made for a smooth and receptive transition and allowed me to feel part of his new position. Wives can use the same method with coaching couples. If he has a difficult time remembering who is married to whom, take pictures at gatherings and play the flash card game. This gives your husband confidence and you the satisfaction of making his job easier.

Active in the Community

Whatever your interest, you can be a fabulous asset to your coach by meeting people in different areas of the community. After Ballinger we moved to Brownwood, Texas. I volunteered for PTA and became involved with the "Just Say No" anti-drug campaign. I loved meeting adults and students throughout the city. Randy promoted the anti-drug theme in athletics, so we were both making the effort to give something back to the community. Many coaches are active with service organizations such as Kiwanis, Rotary, or Lion's Club. Women can join these too!

Expressing Gratitude

Coaches' wives can look at the glass and see "half-full" or "half-empty." Coaching is a business dependent on a lot of support. Giving thanks for the "half-full" glass promotes good feelings. Express your gratitude verbally, send personal notes, send a staff photo Christmas card (to advertisers, administrators, board of trustees, media, etc.), or host a pre- or post-season gathering.

Having an attitude of thanksgiving can spill over to administrators, players, fans, parents, staff coaches, secretaries, custodians, and especially to other coaches' wives! Remember to include the wives of the band director and team doctor. They are also left alone in the stands!

I have always admired Randy's policy of asking his team captains to write thank you notes to the many support groups at school. The faculty certainly appreciates the gesture, but the players who write the notes are the real winners. It is simply good *training!*

Attending Functions

Spending time with your husband often means accompanying him to various events. As we begin to meet other wives and learn to enjoy his sport, it becomes a pleasure to attend games, listen to him speak to the Kiwanis Club, attend banquets and coaching conventions, or even a job interview, if invited!

The first time we are in these social situations, we need to remember little things: don't answer questions for him, don't interrupt, and don't correct him on details. Dress tastefully, smile, be genuine, ask questions about others rather than talking about ourselves. Be a good listener. When someone expresses a concern over something like a sick child, or stressful time ahead, send them a *hand-written* "thinking of you" card.

Relationships With Other Wives on the Staff

The best benefit of all for coaches' wives are other coaches' wives! No one can duplicate these friendships. "Getting along" includes these relationships. When Debbie and Jon Harrison gave us a large, red enamel pitcher for a wedding gift, I did not even know them, but three years later, we were on the same coaching staff in Bryan, Texas. Debbie and I babysat each other's children every week while we attended different Bible studies. Eighteen years later, we are still on the same coaching staff and have traveled countless miles together cheering for our children. We can almost read each other's minds!

Concerning friendships, the questionnaire asked, "How do you feel about your relationship with the other wives on your staff?" and the response was overwhelmingly positive.

- Coaches' wives are the nicest, friendliest women I have met.

- This is one of the most important relationships you can have.

- Wives share so much more than ball games.

As stated in previous chapters, women who understand your particular struggles can be your greatest emotional resource during a time when your husband may be emotionally unavailable.

On the other hand, developing close relationships may take diligence and maturity. Some wives explained that they had difficulties being accepted by the "clique" of wives, especially if they formed themselves into more of a power structure rather than a support structure. There is sometimes jealousy when one husband is promoted over another. Misunderstandings will certainly arise because everyone is human.

However, the thing to remember is that the coaching staff

will be affected by the unity or lack of unity among the wives. One respondent wrote, "I know that if the wives aren't happy with each other, it affects the husbands, too." How could it not? If husbands must "put out the fires" of gossip and jealousy, then their emotional energy is drawn away from the game, but if they are encouraged by seeing their wives help each other, then they have more emotional strength to tackle the stressors of the day. Being in a room with someone who is constantly pointing out the negative aspects of situations is like breathing poisoned air. I want to be an air freshener, not an air poisoner.

One of the greatest benefits of maintaining strong relationships with staff wives is the quiet mentoring that goes on. A more experienced wife explained, "Now that our children are grown, I occasionally help the younger coaches' wives with their little ones. They are so appreciative." A new coach's wife wrote, "Since I'm younger than most of them, they seem like moms to me." This subtle "family" feel creates a safety net for those of us who need to feel both needed and accepted.

The Only Lonely

Responding to the questionnaire, Melanie Simon offered this information, "Currently among Division I-A head football coaches, 6 out of 108 are African-American." Knowing this, it is easy to understand why African-American coaches' wives often find they share a common dilemma. Coaching staffs often employ only one or two black coaches. Hispanics may be in the same situation. Rebecca Hixon explains the anxieties due to racial differences, "It is easy to feel like the 'only lonely' because you are obviously different. Sometimes the only thing you have in common with the other wives is football. It feels awkward when you sense wives are going out of their way to be 'accepting.' "

Rebecca adds advice from other African-American wives:

- Be yourself. Maintain your cultural and ethnic identity. Do not compromise to assimilate into the larger group.

- Get involved in other activities where you can meet other African-Americans.

- Verbalize and share your feelings or frustrations with "majority" wives at the risk of their not understanding. Help them to understand.

- Carve and create your own personal identity. Do not hide your unique talents by focusing just on your husband's job.

- Don't always focus on the negatives and miss out on the fun parts of being involved in this profession.

The Black Coaches' Association is a great source of support for African-American coaches and their wives. For information on the Black Coaches' Association, call their office in Los Angeles toll free at 1-888-667-3222.

A staff divided will not stand. There are many things which can divide a staff: jealousy, cultural differences, personal values, age, "seniority," finances, habits, children, etc. It is best to keep relationships cordial and not burn bridges.

The coaching profession covers a lot of geographical territory. After being in the coaching ranks several years, everyone seems to know each other, and often they work together again! Diversity is the spice of life. Appreciating our differences can lead to harmony *and* contribute to winning games. And who doesn't want to win more games?

POST GAME COACHING

CHAPTER EIGHT

Unexpected Problems

As Donell Teaff said earlier, most people think the life of a coach's wife is so simple and fun. After all, our husbands only have to work one day out of the week! I, too, was surprised at the complexities of filling this role. Many of the problems we learn through first-hand experience: the long hours required, the physical and emotional demands, and the lack of privacy. Perhaps hearing what the wives in the survey have gone through will help ease the sting.

Absent Husbands

When the coaches' wives responded to the question, "What were some of the unexpected problems you experienced?" the No. 1 answer will not surprise you–**long hours**. It seems that no matter how well-prepared a young wife thinks she is for marriage to a coach, she is still amazed by the time factor involved in this job. A coach's daughter was even surprised. "Although my dad was a coach, and I knew how many hours he spent working, it was different when my husband was putting in those long hours. Those hours seemed much longer."

Often a wife feels as though the job is a thirsty sponge that soaks up her husband's attention as well as his time. A wife explained, "In the beginning, it was hard for me when Rick would come home and not want to talk. He would say, 'I've been talking all day long–I'm too tired to talk any more.'" Perhaps some of you have had this difficult experience. Not only is he often away from home, but when he is physically home, he may be emotionally absent.

Single Parenting

A natural result of physically and emotionally absent husbands is the void felt in parenting. Coaches' wives understand the challenges of single parenting while still being married. For the wives who looked forward to the traditional marriage (the wife does the dishes, clothes, shopping, etc. and the husband does the car, plumbing, home repairs, etc.), being responsible for everything during his season is a challenge. Joe Sarah Harrell remarked, "Since our marriage, I have become a pretty good 'handy woman' and know all the local repair shops. I also know my daddy's phone number."

An even greater distress to wives during their husband's coaching season is the difficulties experienced by their children. I can usually forgive someone who hurts me easily, but when my children are hurt, that is a different story. What if the one hurting my children is their father, and there is little he can do about it? What happens when birthdays are missed and promises are broken? What happens when children begin to act out in school in order to gain more attention, and you know the root of the problem is your husband's absence?

It's pretty hard to replace Dad all the time. It is awkward to be the only link between your children's experiences and their dad. Every evening feels like catch up when you are trying to keep him informed about events in their day. I did my best to foster quality time between Randy and the children. We would go to practices, pep rallies, and sometimes take a picnic supper to him at the field house. To this day, we can sing all the words to many fight songs! Our birthdays are in May and June, so that made it easy for him to be there. (Of course, they weren't planned that way–any coach's wife worth her salt knows to plan for Fall babies so you don't have to hold them back a grade. Summer birthdays can be a disadvantage, maturity wise.)

During their elementary grade years, Randy may have missed some things, but I found that the kids were fine if *I* had a good attitude about his absence. During middle school and high school, Wednesday nights became "date night" for Ashley and her dad. They would get pizza and talk. During hectic times when these dates were skipped, I could tell a difference in Ashley. Because he played football, Zac naturally lived in Randy "zone."

There may be times that you will want to call the head coach and ask for your husband to be off for an important event, but let your husband do the asking. Some head coaches are more approachable than others, but the issue here is that the other coaches will give your husband a hard time if *you* do the asking.

The respondents to the survey also indicated that they were surprised at the special difficulties a coach's daughter experiences. In a previous chapter, a daughter discussed how she rarely had dates because the boys feared her father. Daughters also indicated that they experienced an extra dose of jealousy from other girls because the coach's daughter often knows the athletes better and is better prepared to compete in her own sports, as well as cheerleading.

Emotional Demands

Before a wife can adequately deal with the emotional demands produced by her position, she must first become secure in her relationship with her husband. I'm not sure why, but women seem to constantly test the heart of the man they love. "Just how much does he love me?" Consciously and subconsciously, wives continuously look for the answer. If you could get them to be honest with you, most wives would say that there is something that they feel they play "second fiddle" to: a car he's fixing up (as soon as that one is done, he buys another one), the TV, golf, his "whatever" collection, his "whatever" hobby. Wives often say to themselves, "If it came down to a choice between me and 'whatever', the 'whatever' would win." For coaches' wives, the "whatever" is their sport(s). One wife lamented, "After the first few years of marriage, my husband's 'first love' became football. That's still very hard to accept."

Whether or not you do, indeed, play "second fiddle" to his sport is immaterial; the issue is whether you feel and act like a second fiddle. Remember this rule: Blessed is the coach's wife who doesn't make him choose between loving you and loving his sport. There are always exceptions and difficult situations, but under normal circumstances, there is no need for an ultimatum. If you are willing to lean into the difficulty instead of running away from it, then his love for you and his work will become so intertwined that he honestly cannot imagine being able to do his beloved job without his beloved wife. Instead of competing, contribute, and you'll gain more of the love and attention that you desire.

Once a wife is secure with herself, she is better equipped to deal with the pain brought to her husband. The respondents to the survey indicated that they were surprised at the emotional devastation their husbands experienced after losing an important game, or playing through a losing season, or being the focus of cruel criticism. When the coach comes home and stares at the wall, yells at you and the kids, or retreats to the garage, you are at a loss. Wives desperately want to "fix" the hurt, smooth and heal what is wounded, but we often don't have a clue, especially during the early years, about how to respond.

Most of us simply have to learn through experience. The best response may be to just be quiet. Our first instinct is to get our husbands to talk about their feelings because that is what most of us would do, and talking often helps us. Most husbands need just the opposite–quiet. Instead of talking through their feelings, they think through them. Some of them yell through them, and as long as the yelling doesn't become abusive, it may be best just to let him yell without correcting what he is saying. "Now, Honey, you know that you don't really want to kill that kid" isn't helpful. If you're married to a ranter and if he isn't cruel and if you let him rant, chances are he won't even remember what he said the next day if you don't remind him of it, and he'll actually feel better. If you are married to someone who responds to pain by retreating and being quiet, you will actually prolong the pain by trying to force him to talk to you. He will come back to you quicker emotionally if you let him have his time alone. He might even share what he's been thinking about if he feels that you are not going to analyze or correct him. When your husband hurts, be careful about trying to dissect his feelings for him: "Well, I think you feel this way because of what your father said when you were five." They just don't want to hear it.

It is true that their egos are fragile, and they often hinge their own self-worth on the next game or the next season. I'm not sure that a wife can change that; however, she can make him feel so secure in her presence that he needs never pretend around her and need never feel that his "contract" with her is in jeopardy.

Irate Fans

A new coach's wife who is unfamiliar with the athletic world is naturally surprised, even shocked, at the behavior of some fans who seem to take the sport so seriously; it is as though their next paycheck depended upon a win. However, even the experienced coach's wife who has grown up around the overly-serious, hypercritical, irrational fans, finds the situation difficult to deal with when the anger of the "fans" is directed towards her husband. She knows the work involved in preparing the player, how patient her husband has to be with unreasonable parents, and athletes who barely passed classes in order to participate. She knows the diplomacy he must practice in order to maintain unity on the coaching staff. She knows about the "quirks of fate" that could have changed the outcome of the game. Had Earl not torn his knee, Jason not moved away right before the season, Chris not gotten into trouble the day of the game–the fans don't take these into consideration when *they* want to win.

The wives in the survey indicated that they learned how to

handle their feelings about irate fans through experience. Notice that I didn't say that they learned how to handle the fans; they learned how to handle their feelings. The majority of fans are supportive and kind as long as they feel that the players (their children, nephews, friends) are being treated fairly, but nothing can be done for irrational fans. Often, if they are ignored, they calm down in a few days and/or simply find something else to complain about. If they decide that they just don't like your husband, their mind may be made up; no amount of explaining can change that, so don't waste your breath.

If the fans ruin the game for you, do what this wife did: "I just removed myself and sat some place by myself. As I matured, I was able to put it in perspective. Now I can handle it when they get onto my husband."

What about anonymous letters? Ask your husband how he wants them treated. At our house, I open all letters that do not carry a return address. If it's an anonymous letter, I toss it and do not mention it to Randy. He does not want the distraction.

Parent Problems

Although every coaching couple expects to have disagreements and frustrating moments with parents, few are prepared to deal with lawyers hired by parents to "make sure" that their children are treated fairly. Times have changed and occasionally, the pressure on a coach is so strong that he can barely focus on the job at hand. Sometimes "politics" becomes the focus rather than the sport; administrators, under pressure from "parents with power" offer suggestions about the line-up for the next game or the positions certain players might hold the next season.

Perhaps the greatest pressure of all on a coach and his wife is knowing that, no matter how hard he tries to do his job with integrity, some parents and other members of the community will still think he is the devil's cousin who is out to harm their child and their school. A respondent to the survey remarked on the insensitivity of those who spewed "verbal attacks on the coaching staff in the bleachers while my children were with me."

It takes courage and maturity to deal with others in a coaching situation. One wife learned a tough lesson. "I have always taken people at face value, and if they acted like my friend, I thought they were. After my husband became a head coach, I saw this wasn't always true."

Public Life

The wives responding to my survey said that they were always equally surprised with the demands made on them by the public. If you live in a fairly large town, the coach's wife may actually be invisible. Few may know your name and even fewer may know that you exist and you may or may not like it that way. Those who live in a larger town actually get to choose how much of the spotlight they desire.

However, if you're the coach's wife in a small town, everyone may know what you "once considered private information." Any personal topic is considered fair game at the drug store coffee shop where all the city business takes place. And remember, everyone seems to be related, so be careful whom you criticize. During our years in a small town, we spent several weeks in the summer living in Bryan while Randy worked on his master's degree at Texas A&M. It provided the best of both worlds: it gave us a chance to visit with old friends, and then anticipate our return to the benefits of our small town. Living in a small town provided some of our fondest memories. The people are genuinely appreciative. They are generous with their time and energy. I'll never forget 10:00 a.m. on Fridays: radio station KRUN broadcasts the pep rallies. Everyone in town was tuned in and wearing their red and black.

One thing that small and large communities have in common, however, is that they both consider your husband public property. "Don't our taxes pay his salary?!" may be their perspective, giving them the "right" to interrupt your dinner in a restaurant, your evening home alone, and even your prayers at church. I learned this as a young coach's wife. One evening before Randy arrived home, a player's parents came by to talk. Bad mistake. Once Randy arrived, the mother turned on the tears, "He's been on the all-stars every year, and now he never gets to play..." After that, I directed all parent calls at home to his conference period at the office.

A particularly uncomfortable aspect of being public property is having the coaches' salaries published in the newspaper. One wife who experienced this said, "People cannot help but compare, and it causes some bad feelings."

Moving

The number of times they were expected to move also topped the list as an unexpected problem. Sure, they knew that moving was part of the job, but some families seem to stay perpetually packed. For example, Larry and Sandy Brown have been married 24 years, have three children, and have lived in 25 different homes. In a later chapter, I'll discuss moving in more detail, but many are surprised at the number.

Unexpected Problems for the Coach

Only after Randy turned 40 did we find out how common skin cancer is in the coaching profession. What happened to those youthful coaches with the bronze muscles? If they didn't protect themselves with sunscreen (and few did), they now are seeing skin cancer on their ears, nose and arms. Encourage your coach to wear sunscreen, wide brimmed hats, good sunglasses, and stay alert to skin changes.

Sleepless nights can also be a problem. Many a coach wakes up on the couch, or leaves at 4:30 a.m. to go to the office when stress is at a peak. I have tried to make our bedroom particularly serene and comfortable for this reason. We have a net canopy, feather topper on the mattress, fans and a sleep machine to soothe the noise in the room. Of course, I can't solve all his problems this way!

The last problem I wasn't prepared for were Randy's stress-induced allergies. When I least expect it, he sneezes so forcefully that I almost get angry. This only happens during the season. After trying cortisone shots and medications, we found a solution. Randy gets half-hour massages weekly in the fall. (I'm glad his massage therapist is named Charles.) It's amazing how much it has helped his allergies.

The Bible says, "In the day of prosperity, be joyful, and in the day of adversity, consider: God has made one as well as the other" (Ecclesiastes 7:13). I wonder if Solomon knew the myriad of problems a coach's wife would face! No matter what you encounter, realize that you are not alone! Through the long hours without your coach, screaming fans, invasions of privacy, moves, and adjustments, *consider* the strength available to you through family, friends, and the Lord.

CHAPTER NINE

Intangible Rewards

When asked about the rewards for coaches, one wife asked, "Are there *any?*" Of course, coaches' wives *are* the richest women on earth! Sure, some positions offer great perks, but the intangibles are the best of all.

At reunions, have you noticed that the men flock to the coaches? They would give anything to trade in their office job for the thrill of coaching a team. They quiz the coach, "What kind of team do you have coming back next year?" because the coach is connected to the future.

Coaching couples are always sowing seeds for the next generation. They may not live in a mansion, but the seeds bring forth a beautiful garden of friendship and respect, and the rewards are reaped for years to come.

The Reward of Relationships

- Being a best friend to Sam is my greatest reward. I know there are times I am the only one he can talk to honestly, and this has strengthened our relationship.

- I have been grateful to the many other coaches' wives

I've made friends with, and feel a special bond to, because of coaching life.

- The biggest reward to me is seeing the young people we have been involved with, years later. We have been invited to many class reunions and it is wonderful to see the families and hear the stories of their lives. This past August we attended a 30-year reunion and it was so good to know men and women still cared enough to want to see us.

- Rewards come and go with the seasons. A young coach's wife may think that during a big winning season, she has acquired many new friends. It only takes a long dry spell to dispel those misconceptions.

- My biggest reward is the close relationships I have with the athletes. I'm their second mom. I laugh and cry with them.

- The games bring our family closer together. My in-laws travel from Pennsylvania to Ohio every weekend!

The Reward of Making a Difference

- I know that my husband has touched many young people's lives and given them values they may not have had otherwise.

- When a young man he coached a couple of years ago tried to commit suicide Rick wrote him a long letter. That boy wrote back thanking him for remembering him though he no longer coached him.

- One year we got a letter from a kid he had coached, saying, "Coach, I didn't even like you when you were my coach, but I wanted you to know you are the only person in my life that taught me how to work and I'm a success now. Thanks."

The Reward of Respect

- People don't need for you to prove anything to them. They look up to you in a sense. People appreciate what you and your husband do for the kids.

- The admiration and respect his players and students show him is worth more than money in the bank.

- His name opens doors for me and provides the ability to have a positive impact on whatever I undertake.

- Seeing high school boys pat your husband on the back—even when we lose. We had three players come to our house at 11:30 one Friday night after a disappointing loss, just to check on Coach—that's a special reward.

- Seeing my children proud of their Daddy makes me smile.

Sharing The Highs

- The look in my husband's eyes when the boys achieve a goal is priceless.

- There is nothing more exciting than a packed stadium on a Friday night and the support that the team and the coaches get from the community.

- I love listening to Friday night and Saturday scores so I can rejoice and empathize with other coaches' wives I know.

- Once, Steve was speaking at the All Sports Banquet and he said that he wanted to recognize the "wind beneath his wings" and told me that he loved me and appreciated me in front of all those men!! It was one of the greatest moments of my life.

- You share in the excitement of victory. You also see the spiritual growth of the young athletes.

The Extras!

- I think it helps keep you in touch with today's world by being in touch with the young people.

- We never have to worry about getting bored.

- Getting into the games free!

- Since my husband coaches at a U.S. military academy, we get to shop in the commissary!

- Charter flights to playoff games.

Drum Beats and Heart Beats

You've experienced the thrill of hearing the band playing the fight song. The drumbeat seems to match the pounding of your heart! The action is about to start! You get the picture: sitting with loved ones, seeing cousins and grandparents who drove in for the game, end zone games being played during Daddy's game, heroes in the making, feeling a part of something big. The coaching life has its own special rewards.

TO UNPACK OR NOT TO UNPACK, THAT
IS THE QUESTION.

CHAPTER TEN

Moving

How many times have you been driving down the highway next to an overloaded U-Haul and your husband says, "Must be an old secondary coach that got beat deep one time too many"? We joke about waking up to moving vans and "For Sale" signs. After a bad season, one coach actually had a load of dead fish dumped on his front lawn.

No matter what the reason for moving (promotion, staff changes, "conflict of philosophy"), it is *tough!* Coaching is a *mean* business. If the move comes after months of criticism or after being fired, there is a grieving and healing process that must take place. For being in such a "tough guy" profession, coaches and their confidence are very fragile. It takes a strong and sensitive wife to build up her coaching husband. We are a team when we win and a team when we lose.

Physical Demands

Ideally, the new team that has hired your husband will sell your home and send movers to do all the work for you. Realistically, you get to do-it-yourself. Since your husband is focusing on the details and demands of his new job, you can easily end up doing the packing, selling, calling, cleaning, and hauling if you are not careful to communicate your needs. Perhaps you can divide the list of things to be done: "Honey, I will pack and clean the house if you will bring the boxes home early and do the loading and take the trash. I can have a garage sale to eliminate some things we don't need and make some extra money. Will you take care of closing our accounts?"

One resource to consider is "Movemasters, Inc." I have not personally used their service but became acquainted with it at a coaching convention. This company specializes in helping coaches sell homes, find homes, manage property, handle household goods, and more. Their phone is 800-452-0337. Ask for Tom Lyddy.

Before the task of moving is at your doorstep, organize your household and take advice from those who have blazed the trail. Wives experienced in moving (the average moves was 5!) offered the following advice for those new to the game:

- Try to get the cost of the move included in your contract.

- Start moving early. Use the post office to mail boxes on set dates. Get a quick feel for the community and what they expect of you through several short visits there.

- Try not to accumulate too much junk. Pack carefully. Weed out what you don't need.

- Don't move alone. Get help from other coaches and students.

- Use small to medium sized boxes because they are easier to handle by yourself. Your coach may be unable to be there when you actually move your possessions. Remember to keep those boxes for the next move that may be around the corner.

- Don't unpack everything! Plan to move next year again even if you don't.

- Never buy good furniture. It's always the first to get damaged in moving.

Other Considerations

1. *Time of Year* - if there is a choice, it is great to move in early spring so everyone can get settled before the summer. This will allow for a return to normalcy before the season begins!

2. *Housing - buy or rent?* - Financial consultant, Russ Crosson, explains the variables to consider in his book, *A Life Well Spent.* In general, he says, buy if you are sure to live in a house at least two years. Otherwise, rent. Randy and I know coaching couples who have chosen to rent while investing in a lake home. They have a place to escape to and will have a place to retire.

3. *Location* - Ask a school administrator's wife to drive you around and ask for her advice.

4. *Recruit Assistance* (muscle power) from the staff and players there. This is a good bonding experience.

5. *Write down a plan* of attack for organizing your new domicile! Again, agree on a his and hers list, even a kids list so all the work doesn't fall on you. Don't assign the coach a job that has to be completed too soon!

6. *Decorating* - Coaches' wives are the most resourceful creatures on earth at making a house become a home. Team colors rule! Don't throw away that tattered bedspread in your child's room. Piece together large checked gingham in a school color and cover it!

Emotional Demands

Most of us get attached to our church, co-workers, doctor, grocery store, and our familiar routine, but when our coach says, "It's time to move on," we begin making adjustments. Our emotions run the spectrum–anger, resentment, fear, impatience, curiosity, excitement.

Some moves may be easy. You're ready to leave that "crummy little town" or you're ready for a simple change of scenery. Perhaps you enjoy the excitement of a new place and starting over. Sometimes the moves are painful. You may have deep ties with a particular location or group of people. In this case, don't be afraid to grieve the loss. You may not be able to respond "perfectly" every time the U-haul arrives, but you have not failed as long as you continue to courageously *lean into* the problem and seek to *resolve* the hurt instead of becoming bitter.

Psychologist Patricia Decker says, "Most of us struggle with endings. We tend to take them too seriously (Throw back your head, bring your arm across your forehead and shriek, 'This is the end!') or blow them off ('Let's not talk about the past, OK, Babe?'). Yet, it is endings which make beginnings possible. The gray area between endings and beginnings may seem barren and empty, but there's a lot of growth going on just beneath the surface."

Listen to the advice from other coaches' wives on the emotional aspect of moving:

- No place is perfect, so stop looking.

- Never say "I'll never move again." Find a bright side to the move and don't look back. We have very dear friends that we still visit, from every place we have lived.

- Trust in the Lord and don't get too attached to possessions.

- Don't burn your bridges behind you because you may return to the same district.

- One of the first things you need to do is find a church home.

- Moves are fun when the children are young, but very difficult for older children.

- Bloom where you are planted.

- Be patient. It takes a while to feel at home.

- Decide to like it before you move.

- Every place is different. Every staff is different. Don't always compare and expect things to be a certain way.

Returning to His Alma Mater

When Randy and I moved back to his home town, a television station interrupted "Wheel of Fortune" to make the announcement. We were told to keep it a secret, because the teams needed to be told first. We had not even told Randy's parents when they heard it on a special news bulletin. What a crazy profession!

Many coaches have a goal to revive his alma mater. Moving back reunites him with family, friends, memories, and loyalties. Can a coach go home again? Yes, but the tough part is accepting the inevitable changes.

Starting Over

Coaches' wives are not alone when it comes to making emotional adjustments. Susan Miller, author of *After the Boxes Are Unpacked*, helps explain the dilemma and process of this transition. I highly recommend it. One chapter lists the advantages of moving to a new location:

You have a chance to start over.

You will be known for the person you are today, not the person you were in the past.

You have more control of your time because you don't have old commitments.

Nobody has seen your wardrobe.

You may find time to break old habits.

Moving will broaden your horizons and allow you to experience a new culture.

Before you get too involved with other things, you can renew and revitalize your relationship with God.

Good Luck!

CHAPTER ELEVEN

Finances

How does your coach spell "Success"?

M-O-N-E-Y or W-I-N-S?

We all know the answer! While husbands in other professions are investing in Wall Street, our husbands are investing in the lives of young people. These dividends are far more valuable and can last forever! However, a coaching family can suffer when real financial issues are neglected.

It takes a great amount of discipline and communication to manage a small salary–especially when the job requires long hours, frequent moves, and demands a high profile.

I don't feel I am the best person to be giving advice in this category! Randy manages 22 coaches' budgets; therefore, I handle the budget at home. As long as I keep my priorities straight, I do fine. My weaknesses are travel (short overnight trips) and clothes.

Barbara Shealy, mother of five, and survivor of 10 moves, says, "The coach is too busy to pay bills and does not assume enough responsibility to encourage a savings account or plans for retirement. I see finances being a big issue in marriages. The husbands need to shop more with their wives—it's a shock to them sometimes to see how much it costs for food and clothes and how many needs there are when raising a family—and how fast a paycheck can be depleted."

When coaches' wives were asked about their unique financial concerns, many rightly expressed dismay over the lack of compensation their husbands receive, considering the amount of time and energy they give to their jobs. A wife commented, "One time we figured it out. Rick put in so many hours that it added up to only 25 cents per hour. We learned not to spend money that we didn't have." Occasionally telling your husband that he is underpaid for the work he does may make him feel appreciated, but if he hears it too often, he may believe that you are complaining about his ability to provide for the family. Another wife gave some excellent advice about keeping finances in perspective: "You do have to plan and spend wisely. As long as you live within your means, you'll be okay. Try to stay out of debt and keep your material possessions light; it makes moving much less of a hassle." She's right. For the family whose taste is simple, who places more value on the intangible rewards, and who practices self-discipline in spending, a coaching salary will meet their needs under normal circumstances.

Moving Gets Expensive!

Moving can be a financial killer. Like Christmas, moving is inevitable and requires financial preparation to avoid unwanted debt. Coaches' wives both laugh and cry about this subject. Deposits, movers, and bills to be paid off in one location so they are not carried on to the new location are just a few of the

headaches. If the wife stays to sell the house, the coach has living expenses in the new city. If the wife moves before the house
sells, two house payments may be required from the monthly
paycheck. It's often a financial Catch 22.

Coaches' wives universally agree that the financial aspect of
moving is one of the most difficult parts about coaching. They
gave this advice:

- Save, save, save.

- Don't be extravagant.

- You can make any house a home. Keep your payments low
  and always consider resale.

- Trust God.

The Boring Budget

The way a couple manages finances usually reflects their
personality as well as their values. The couples with "perfect"
financial records and substantial savings are also the ones who
iron their sheets and manicure their lawns. Others may not even
know what they make, much less be able to figure out a budget
or plan for upcoming bills. "Budgets" in the strictest sense of the
word are difficult to create, and most people rarely follow them.
They are akin to diets. We know we should do it, and most people stay with it a while, but sooner or later, it's just no fun, and
we quit. The general rule of thumb is to find a method that you
are comfortable with, one that you can and will use. Instead of

formulating complicated budgets, most money managers agree on the following ideas:

1. Decide on your most important financial priorities and have those payments automatically deducted from your check. For example, if you wish to start a "moving fund," and you feel you can miss $25 a month, have it deducted *before* you even see your check. The same is true for retirement, college, etc. The most important principle is to *pay yourself first*, and the easiest way to do it is through automatic deductions.

2. Always save **something** from each paycheck. Most advisors agree that it is best to save on a percentage basis. If your finances are tight, start with 1%. Put that much in savings from *every* paycheck. Periodically increase the percentage. If you get a 3% pay increase, add another percentage to your savings. If you move to another job and the paycheck increases 10%, increase your savings by 4% and so on.

3. Another general principle is to always allow each spouse spending money for which they do not have to account–even if it is just $5. That "walking around money" can give a person a sense of control that he/she needs to make it through tough financial times.

4. Decide on a dollar amount for discussing purchases. I know some couples who decided that anything over $25 needs to be discussed. Some families in less critical situations set the amount at $100. This will give both parties a chance to consider a decision, and it reduces "impulse" buying.

5. Do your best to live below your means. I know that may be impossible early in your marriage, but advisors agree that people do not gain security living *within* their means. Only by living *below* it can you invest and save for the future. You may be *able* to afford a $40,000 car, but if a $20,000 car works, choose it. You may be able to afford an $80,000 home, but if a $50,000 home will do the job, choose it.

Help With the Budget

Budgeting may be boring, but it can actually improve your marriage. The necessary communication causes us to be honest with each other. Randy and I began using the Quicken computer program. It relieves the pressure of one person saying, "No, you can't buy that," because the computer displays the numbers. I can't argue with the computer! It has been a great program in helping us stick to our goals.

An excellent financial planning program has been designed for the American Football Coaches Association. Written by Robert V. Courtet, Jr. of Atlanta, Georgia, the workbook states:

The coach's wife, as in all family matters, is a **pivotal** factor in the success of the family's financial well-being. She is the most ,important financial counselor a coach could have. Wives have already learned to be a team player in a coach's professional career, so they know the concept. They are also team players when it comes to the investment game plan for the family. They must work together with their husbands to understand the entire financial planning picture. The wives of coaches are in a position to take on responsibilities, making it easier for their husbands to focus on their coaching career.

Courtet also emphasized the importance of coaching couples finding a good financial counselor. Because every couple's situation is unique, there are no absolute answers. However, every couple who is willing to set honest and realistic goals together can reach them!

Who makes a good financial counselor?

1. Someone recommended by a trusted friend.

2. A non-relative.

3. A professional who will be able to keep up with your goals after you move from that location.

High-Profile Image

Let's face it—another financial pressure on coaches is to look good. They are in a high profile position regardless of the coaching level. At a small middle school or in the college ranks, coaches are looked up to by students and adults. Therefore, they are expected to exude an image that commands respect. Often that is interpreted as "quality" clothes, living in an upper-middle class neighborhood, and driving a luxury car. Coaching couples and their children feel the nudge to keep up with their friends and community members whose salaries are substantially higher.

Those families who give in to this pressure often find that it is a bottomless pit because a certain house requires certain furniture. A certain neighborhood requires a country club membership and a certain school which will require that your children dress a certain way. You see, it never stops. Once a person decides to live his life by the standards of others, he is in danger of losing his self-worth entirely.

An experienced coaching couple soon learns that a coach gains respect

from . . .	not from . . .
A healthy, clean physique	New, expensive clothes
Devotion to wife and family	A big home in the "right neighborhood"
A disciplined lifestyle	A luxury car

Integrity and courage rate higher than flamboyance. One coach was not hired after his reference said, "He can't pay his bills." If this hits home with you, get a copy of your credit history and work to clean it up. It really is a good idea for everyone to check his credit periodically. Once, when we applied for a home mortgage, we found out that another person with my husband's name was on our credit report.

Learning From Others

A Life Well Spent by Ross Crosson is a book that will help you with financial decisions. It is geared toward helping families delicately and effectively balance earning power and family time.

It answers when to buy or rent, when to buy a new car, when the wife should work, etc.

Coaches' wives are the most resourceful creatures on the planet! Redecorating a rental house on a shoestring is their specialty!

Sandy Sobeck offers these creative ideas: "We have used the envelope system for groceries. Money is divided for weeks one through four. It causes me to plan ahead and be more disciplined. Also, we treat college savings as though we are paying a bill. Our baby-sitting expenses were solved by joining a trusted baby-sitting co-op. It has helped my boys and myself meet new friends."

Teammates!

If you are already a good money manager–congratulations! It is a wonderful discipline. If, however, financial pressures are part of your marriage, I hope you no longer feel alone. Sharing your coach's vision for young people doesn't mean your family has to suffer. Seek advice from suggested books, church and community seminars, or from a trusted professional.

Work together as teammates on a game plan to reach your goals!

COACH'S WIFE ON GAME DAY

CHAPTER TWELVE

The Seasons —
Winning and Losing

Anticipation. It's the electricity that runs through every coaching family before the season begins. Last year is over. Hopes are high for this one. All of the mundane hours of the off-season practice, videos, clinics, weight-training classes are complete, and like a trumpet in a silent field, a new season is announced. The coach goes into his "zone." He will not be the same person for four or five months, but we love him anyway.

Remember in the movie *Hoosiers* when the coach defends Jimmy's passion for playing? He says, "You know, most people would kill to be treated like a god just for a few moments!" Our husbands have felt that rush, that high, and they seek it again each new season. That's why they're in coaching.

To the coach's wife, a new season brings mixed emotions: excitement and emptiness. There's the excitement of sharing the coach's dream. I get caught up in the spirit of the season. We have "Cougar" bank checks; I wear "Cougar" earrings; our front door has a football door knocker; and Randy has a complete wardrobe of football ties. But there is also a sense of emptiness because we know our husbands will be "detached" for the season. Teenager Maureen Kyle describes her dad as going into a daze and walking around "mumbling to himself. We'll find plays all over the place, little X's and O's on envelopes."

Concerning life, love, and marriage, a counselor once said, "Anything that has the potential for great joy and promise also has the potential for great sorrow and defeat." This statement is especially applicable to the coach and his family. The wins produce a joy that few experience, and the losses bring sorrow and a time of great pressure.

It was like following Bear Bryant when Randy followed Gordon Wood (500 career wins) at Brownwood High School. Our son was in third grade. His Sunday school teacher, Cherry Sharpe, asked the class, "Can anyone tell me what is Zac's daddy's job?" A boy named Matt jumped and waved his hand high and said, "I know what his job is. It is TO WIN!" Now that's pressure.

The Wins

Here's how coaches' wives describe their winning seasons:

- Winning seasons are like tightrope walking. Everyone is so intense they're afraid to take a deep breath.

- We won 14 straight games four years in a row. We were State champs in 1991 and married the day after the State Championship game. It was great.

- I opened a new elementary 10 years ago, and I told my fourth and fifth graders when they were varsity players our high school would go to the playoffs (it was a new school, too). When my fifth graders were juniors, we did it for the very first time. What a feeling.

- Our football season goes on so long, we're all exhausted, but on such a high. We are truly running on adrenaline. Each week in the playoffs the town tries to do something special for the team and tries to top what they did the week before. It is awesome!!

The Losses

Sprinkled into every coach's career are the losses. They are necessary to keep our men humble and hungry, but they can be so painful. They cause a coach to lose confidence. The coach's wife can feel very helpless. Melanie Simon aptly describes the morning after a loss as a "Football Hangover." Other wives describe it this way:

- When we lose, stress is rampant and extends to all family members. My heart breaks for him and I want to know how to help.

- There's good news and bad when you speak about losing. The good news first: the season is shorter. The bad news is that it's never short enough!

- Losing seasons are tough because the kids hurt so much, and the coaches seem to try even harder to figure out what they can do to change the situation. I worry that people won't hang in there long enough for the tide to turn. You know it will, but you just hope they have patience until it builds and gets going.

- You really find out who your real friends are.

- We went from the Penthouse to the Outhouse!! The year after making it to the semifinals for the third time we moved and my husband became a Defensive Coordinator. We went 1-9. I thought it couldn't get any worse. It did! We had a player die on the sidelines. I never say, "It can't get any worse."

- The last two years we've gone 3-7. As Forrest Gump says, "That's all I have to say about that."

The End of the Season

The end of the season is ticklish. Wives who have been "holding back" and "keeping in" and "stuffing down" feelings, needs, and desires have secret hopes of "unloading" on their man the day after the season ends. They even think they are being generous by waiting until the next day. After all they have "suffered" for months. Now, it's time to turn some of the responsibility back over to him. Let him pay the bills, discipline the kids, and take care of the car repairs. On top of that, he had better be planning some pretty romantic evenings; after all, he owes his wife a few!

However, experienced wives have learned that even though the season is technically over, it is not emotionally over for the coach. Remember this rule: For the coach, every season is a losing season unless he wins it all. Now that may not make a bit of sense to you because you know that he said, "I'll be satisfied if we just win district." Yes, he said it, but that doesn't **matter because any season is a losing season if he doesn't win it all.** Therefore, after the last game is played, the coach needs time to grieve.

Our family has a tradition of "escaping" after that last game. Immediately, we go out of town to a fun spot. It breaks Randy away from the routine, the media, even the well-meaning church friends who say, "Good season, Coach." It reknits our family. It gives him time to verbalize or silently re-evaluate the season. We always come home refreshed.

One November we drove five hours to Sea World! We had a great time as a family, yet I noticed that during the shows, Randy would drop his head and replay the game in his mind. I knew he was second guessing plays he had called that could have changed the outcome. Some coaches blame the players if they lose, but Randy always shoulders the loss personally. It may sound as though the time was gloomy, but it wasn't. We still laughed and appreciated just being together even if his mind was somewhere far away.

Another season, Randy arranged for the use of a condominium in New Mexico at Thanksgiving. It broke family tradition, but provided fresh healing scenery for Randy. The four of us had a wonderful time skiing and watching movies.

Last year's escape in Dallas came after a Cinderella season. We lost in the state finals in Texas Stadium. The next day we wanted to visit friends, but Randy only had his stale coaching clothes from the night before. What would any self-respecting woman do? Get *him* a makeover! I talked him into going to Nordstrom and with a "Bibbity-bobbity-boo" he was transformed into a normal person again: new shirt, slacks, socks, shoes, and belt! Being the week of Christmas, it was the perfect gift. He actually *acted* like a new person, too! I highly recommend this escape.

The Media

The coaches that live in a community with a positive media should count their blessings! There are some fabulous, supportive men and women in television and the press who love promoting athletics. Coaches recognize the "good ones" and give a lot of precious season time to give quotes. A supportive newspaper can provide the ingredients for a wonderful scrapbook. And guess who gets to cut out the articles and put it together? We enjoy seeing their efforts appreciated.

When our team is overlooked or criticized, we want to call up that sportswriter and tell him off! We want to write anonymous letters! Go ahead and write that letter–but tuck it in your desk drawer for a week and let the emotion fade. Then throw the letter away.

In 20 years I've seen only a couple letters to the newspaper written by coaches' wives. Even if trying to be positive, it is better to not make an issue of ourselves. I've often used the rule, "If in doubt, don't."

I suppose dealing with the media is a subject for the *coach,* rather that the coach's wife; however, we can help our husbands and ourselves by learning how to have a good relationship with the media. I recommend an excellent audio cassette series called "Winning with the Media" by sportscaster Andrea Kirby. On two tapes, she gives practical insights on how to develop good communication skills and take control of one's career with the media. The address is listed in the bibliography.

Wives answering my survey presented clear views on how to maintain a positive attitude toward the game while dealing with the media.

- I get really tired of the constant phone calls during the season but know it is necessary to maintain a good relationship. I don't always like or agree with what they write or say, but realize I have no control over other people's attitudes–only mine toward them."

- I guard my tongue and smile a great deal.

- Anything positive I cut out and frame. Anything negative gets thrown away.

- I've learned that when you're winning, the kids get the credit. When you're losing it's "that stupid coach." I know he is a great man, my kids know he's a great man, and that's all that really matters!

You Can Do It!

Surviving the ups and downs of winning and losing requires an inner strength that takes time and good responses to develop. Experienced wives believe that we can help ourselves if we will follow some simple principles:

1. Take care of yourself by:

• Getting physical rest and eating right. Some days will feel like a battle. A good soldier will not go into battle physically unprepared.

• Stay away from negative people who might drain your emotional energy.

2. Rely on friends, especially other coaches' wives, who can help you keep a positive perspective.

3. Rely on God. Read the Bible and practice its principles. Remind yourself that God's value system has nothing to do with winning or losing games.

4. Remember that change is inevitable!

5. Get involved in helping others. Self pity never builds courage or character. Helping others builds the strength we need to keep ourselves and our families strong.

CHAPTER THIRTEEN

Being Your Best —
Personal Growth and
Looking Good

Coaches are generally in youthful, athletic, and co-ed environments. We have all heard the jokes about the coach who married the high school cheerleader, but hey, chances are you know of a true case! Even though our husbands are surrounded by attractive women, we want our Prince Charming to look forward to coming home to his castle. To be our best, we need to always be maintaining our inner and outward beauty which includes our self-esteem, sense of identity, attractiveness, and wellness.

I'll confess to being an energetic person; however, for two years after Ashley was born, I didn't exercise at all. I was turning into Jello. Our neighbor, Grant Lee, would start his noisy 1962 pickup at 5:00 a.m. and drive to the track to jog. Since that was the only time of day I had a babysitter, I asked Grant if I could tag along. It was so dark that all I could see was the white stripes on the track. I did see a few falling stars. Exercise remains an important part of my routine. I walk on the treadmill, use the stairclimbing machine, and lift hand weights two to three times a week at the YMCA. Out of love and respect for myself, and for Randy, I have always tried to look my best.

Coaches compete for everything from who has the most chest hair to who has the fastest car. When he courted you, your coach believed he was competing for your heart, and when he won it, it was better than winning the Nationals. Now that you, his greatest prize, are secure, he has moved onto other challenges such as winning division and state championships. Consequently, you may feel as though *you* are the one competing for *his* time, attention, and perhaps even *his* heart. On one level this is not true at all. He feels secure in his love for you or else he would not feel free to pursue other goals. On the other hand, you are, indeed, competing with other interests for his day-to-day attention. Therefore, this chapter is about being your best in body, soul, and spirit in order to be attractive to him and yourself.

Self-Esteem

The term "self-image" refers to how I see myself. Do I believe that I am smart, interesting, compassionate, dull-witted, slow, unattractive? Self-image involves the qualities I see as my own. It is also a picture of who I believe I am, including my values, personal experiences and future hopes.

"Self-esteem," however, refers to whether I like what I see. Do I value what I see? Am I important to others? Am I important to myself? What you have heard before is true; if I do not value myself, it is difficult for others to value me as well. If I constantly place myself last in everything, then others begin to think that is where I belong. Now, I know that we have been pushing unselfishness in this book, but there's a difference between unselfishness and martyrdom. On the surface, the "martyr mother" looks as though she is "giving her all" for her family. The truth is that as she gives her all, she often punishes her family through guilt. For example, a teenager asks her mother to take her to the mall, so she can meet some friends for a movie. The mother sighs and does it, but the next day the teen hears, "Well, I had an important doctor's appointment yesterday, but I canceled it because you needed a ride to the movie." This brand of "unselfishness" just creates resentment for all family members.

Joining the "martyr mother" is a wife who has been taking care of others for so long that she honestly doesn't have a clue as to what she wants or needs. She has no dreams, ambitions, or desires. She simply has melted into her children and her husband. Conversations always end with "whatever you want." And she may mean it. Others may initially appreciate her cooperation, but after a while, the wife is no longer asked her opinion when decisions are made because the answer "whatever you want" is always given.

Being unselfish doesn't mean denying your needs. A person with strong self-esteem uses her talents to help others, but she also values herself enough to take care of her needs. I know one teacher whose active family completely filled the summer with so many activities that she was exhausted in August. Finally, at the urging of a friend, she reserved her own week on the calendar, and declared to her family that this week belonged to her. If she wanted to visit with friends or stay in her bedroom eating bonbons and watching "chick flicks," she would. Her husband and teenage children would have to take care of themselves for a while. Although the family was surprised, "Mom's week" became a tradition, and she felt more refreshed starting each new school year.

Your Own Identity

Our husbands receive their identity through their profession. They are simply "Coach." That's why, when he has a losing season, you can say to yourself, "It's just a game," but it doesn't seem to help at all to say that to him. Coaches' wives have a variety of careers, yet their identities and whether they classify themselves as successes or failures depends more on their role as wife, mother, sister, friend, etc. However, if a coach's wife immerses herself so deeply into the world of her husband and children that she forgets to bring along the interests and gifts that are hers, she loses the mystique that makes her attractive.

Jean Lush, a Seattle psychologist, says she is often asked why men have extramarital affairs. The response from the man is that the other woman "stimulates my mind." This reaches far beyond the sexual. Most men initially date a woman out of curiosity. They want to find out who you are beyond what they have seen. When men marry, they are still fascinated by all that there is yet to learn of their wives. However, wives forget to maintain a certain mystique. You may say, "Big deal. I could stimulate his mind, if mine weren't buried under dirty laundry, bills to pay, and game videos." You're right. It's not easy, but it's not always as hard as we think. Keep up with current events, begin a collection, update your computer skills, join an investment club, or try a dance class. You might go back to a hobby that you both enjoyed when you were dating.

If you have time, volunteer in the community or develop a "cause." These interests will help you remember that there is a word: "athletics". Your work with a non-profit organization can also make for more interesting conversations. Mary Barnett and the coaches' wives at Northwestern University began a charity organization called Wildcat Wives to help a local mission. They sell silver Wildcat jewelry to raise funds. I love the Wildcat pin I got from Mary; it looks like our Cougar at Cooper High School. What a fun way for wives on a coaching staff to give to their community *and* promote team spirit!

Learning new skills can also keep us out of the "fish bowl" experience. Gail McDonald, author of *High Call, High Privilege* writes about the need pastor's wives have for maintaining personal growth. She encouraged her readers to expand their scope of reading material, keep a personal journal, learn new crafts, develop computer skills, become a perceptive listener, exercise, etc.

Keeping a journal has been part of my routine for over 12 years. Someone told me that I would forget all the sweet memories of my '30s if I didn't write them down. It keeps me centered and is wonderful therapy.

Looking Your Best

Donell Teaff once told a group of coaches' wives, "Whether you need it or not, get a new robe every year." This is the way your coach sees you.

Looking your best is not about spending a lot of money. Who has money? It is about finding your personal style, exercising, and looking good.

Coaches often stay in a time warp: crew cuts, white socks pulled up over their calves, fishing hats to ward off the sun. Sometimes their players make fun of their style. But every coach wants to be proud of the girl he married—it's that male jock ego.

Don't get me wrong, you're much more to him than a decoration on his arm, and he most likely doesn't expect you to look like Cindy Crawford. But you are part of him which means that if you look sloppy, the world connects him with sloppiness. If you look your best, he not only feels proud but he faces the world with greater confidence. I'm not exactly sure why this is true, but it is.

There are many practical books on the market to help you. Try *Simple Isn't Easy* by Olivia Goldsmith and Amy Fine Collins. (Olivia Goldsmith also wrote *First Wives' Club*). They suggest that a woman pare her wardrobe to the elements which make her feel good about herself. (They even offer a wonderful method for cleaning out your closet!) Once a "uniform" is established, simple items can be added according to style and not fashion trends. After using these ideas for several months, Goldsmith's sister asked her, "You look so nice lately. Have you lost weight?"

Concerning hair (a woman's eternal battle), Goldsmith and Fine state emphatically, "There is no bad hair, only bad haircuts." They suggest looking for a hair dresser that will work to find the best shape for you instead of following fashion trends. They also emphasize the importance of posture. When a woman's hair and clothes look good, she still may look as though she lacks confidence just by the way she stands or sits. "Adopting good posture can make your whole physical presence more attractive," they explain. "It will give the illusion of having confidence and poise, not to mention that your clothes will hang better on you."

Remember *Color Me Beautiful* , the fashion sense book by Carole Jackson that was such a hit in the late 1970's? This book is just as exciting, and it gives fantastic wardrobe strategies that work to help you achieve a simple personal style while saving time and money. Those who follow its principles swear that they save hundreds of dollars by knowing which clothes to avoid, and they end up loving the clothes they buy.

Wellness

Wellness is not about weight, but about fitness. My day job is Coordinator for Personal Health Management, our school district's employee wellness program. Our team travels to each campus to do cardiovascular fitness assessments, give a customized exercise and strength program, and encourage health awareness. Through my work, I see people in all manners of physical condition, and I've learned one thing–it doesn't help to bemoan the terrible shape you're in. Your body may be in pretty good shape and you want to keep it that way. You may be in semi-good shape, or you may feel like the poster child for flab. Whatever the condition, there's only one way to feel better– make one change at a time, one day at a time. Your goal isn't to lose 20 pounds. Your goal is to simply take care of yourself today with a little bit of exercise and some balanced, moderate eating. Keep the goal small, reach it every day, and the larger goal simply takes care of itself.

Besides all of the obvious reasons a family needs to be health conscious, the coaching family needs to pay particular attention because coaches and their families are role models. The players and the community respect a coach who practices what he preaches. Jackie Van Wieren said, "The players often comment on what good shape Coach Van Wieren is in." The kids notice. Some coaches model this better than others, but a coach who has a disciplined lifestyle of good health habits will have a stronger influence on athletes than one who does not. And wives are aware that we have a strong influence on our husband's level of discipline. When we make healthy choices concerning meals and how we spend our time, our husbands tend to follow (primarily because they don't want to make their own dinner!).

Being our best is much more than the superficial kind of beauty that is promoted in the athletic world. As coaches' wives we are beautiful to our husbands when we put forth the effort to stay interesting, attractive, mysterious, healthy, and challenging.

LORD, IF IT BE THY WILL, I PRAY THAT WE WIN THIS GAME BECAUSE HE SURE WILL BE EASIER TO LIVE WITH THIS WEEK.
GO TEAM

CHAPTER FOURTEEN

Faith and FCA

A dynamic dimension in the lives of many coaches' wives is their faith in God. When balancing the emotional, physical, and mental demands–a strong spiritual life can be the difference between giving up and hanging on!

Sometimes it is difficult to see our life from God's divine viewpoint. We know there must be a purpose for all of the people and circumstances that enter our lives. As we turn to Him, He shows us glimpses of that plan.

As an infant, I was blessed into my mother's Jewish faith and baptized into my father's Catholic faith! But at age 16, I felt a void in my life. My friend Tranette explained the gospel to me, that Jesus Christ died on the cross for my sins. By accepting Him as my Savior and believing in Him, God gave me eternal life. My life was never the same. I went to college eager to get involved in Bible studies and meet Christian friends. Working as a counselor at Kanakuk-Kanakomo Kamp, I met a counselor named Randy Allen. Little did I know he was coaching at Bryan High School near my university, Texas A & M. He was handsome, athletic, sensitive, creative, and a mature Christian. He played the guitar and sang his way into my heart. He proposed after we dated only six weeks!

Early in our marriage we began our involvement with the Fellowship of Christian Athletes. What exactly is the FCA? It is a Christian ministry for athletes and coaches headquartered in Kansas City, Missouri. There are state and area offices that assist local clubs, called "Huddles," on the school campuses. Many athletes are first introduced to FCA through their summer Camps held across the nation. It is a session of "inspiration and perspiration," with "celebrity" coaches and athletes as speakers, collegiate athletes as huddle leaders, devotionals, competitions, and stirring music.

Not everyone who reads this book will be comfortable with the Christian aspect of being a coach's wife, but for me and many others who wrote to me, it is difficult to separate this part of our lives. Jesus Christ gives our lives meaning and purpose. He unites us, brings us peace and stability. These verses keep me going:

Colossians 2:6. "As therefore you received Christ Jesus the Lord, so live in him, rooted and built up in Him and established in the faith, just as you were taught, abounding in thanksgiving."

Proverbs 31:10-12. "A wife of noble character who can find? She is worth far more than rubies. Her husband has full confidence in her and lacks nothing of value. She brings him good, not harm, all the days of her life."

Wives expressed repeatedly that their life as a coach's wife cannot be separated from their faith in God:

- I could stop and write a book on this subject. It is more evident everyday that God's hand is in everything we do. We have a much stronger faith. In this profession you had better give your soul to God because the rest of you is anybody's.

- I have learned that God's will takes precedence over our desires for winning.

- Because the coaching profession is so uncertain and unpredictable, I have to trust the Lord for everything. He has always been faithful to meet our needs.

- Sometimes God is the only man in my life. He hears from me daily, good times and bad. My faith has definitely made my marriage and family what it is today.

- I know my husband is not a coach by chance. God put us where we are and I praise God for the opportunities that we have daily. For us, it's mostly walking the walk.

- Being a coach's wife is really no different than being any wife. It is a tough position to play and God's the best coach I've ever had. He loves walk-ons!

FCA

How does FCA involve the coach's wife?

1. Through your husband being a Huddle Coach at his school.

If your husband is the Huddle Coach, there are many ways that you can be involved. FCA meetings often alternate between recreation and speakers. These are ideal family times, depending on the age of your children. Huddle Coaches need assistance with meeting details: place, skits, props, refreshments.

Sometimes the girls like to have a small group Bible study and the coach's wife is an ideal role model, if you have a desire to have a more direct impact and get to know the students. We often forget how real their struggles are.

Randy has started Huddles at each school where he has coached. Leading the music with his guitar has opened many doors. His Huddles have sung at churches, nursing homes, Christmas caroling hayrides, campfires, you name it! For the last six years, he has given the responsibility to a younger coach on the staff. He considers their position as important as the offensive or defensive coordinator's.

2. Through your husband's involvement in an Adult Chapter.

The Adult Chapter consists of men and women in a community who have an enthusiasm for supporting the local FCA Huddles. Adult Chapters often meet at a meal time, share a devotional, update FCA activity around the city, and plan for support. In an effort to unify and strengthen the message of Jesus Christ to all students, Adult Chapters sponsor banquets featuring high profile speakers, and raise funds to scholarship students and coaches to summer Camps. A coach's wife can be blessed through working with the wives of community leaders and praying for the mission of the Adult Chapter.

3. FCA's own newsletter to coaches' wives.

There is a quarterly newsletter for coach's wives called "Behind the Bench." Barbara Shealy, wife of Dal Shealy, president of FCA, began this ministry in 1992. Barbara understands the needs and feelings of a coach's wife. Articles are submitted from wives at all levels, all across the country. "Behind the Bench" is free and available upon request. The address is F.C.A, 8701 Leeds Road, Kansas City, MO 64129. Barbara welcomes *your* articles, too!

4. Taking athletes to summer Camp.

Taking athletes to summer Camp is the perfect way for a coach to spend a family vacation. The Camps are five to six days and located in the most beautiful areas of the country. It is a week of sky-high enthusiasm and activity for the athletes. The families do not have duties, yet can participate and soak in all the sunshine for the soul. It is relaxing to sleep in the dorms or cabins and not cook for a week!

Coaches' kids who have grown up attending summer Camps with their families tell of the profound influence FCA had on their lives as a child: seeing their parents model their love for the students, spending time together as a family in a picturesque setting, and hearing about God from heroes.

5. Attending a Coach's Camp as a couple.

Created to energize the coaching couple, FCA Coaches' Camps are retreats that help open rapport and offer spiritual and emotional support. FCA recognizes the strain that coaching puts on marriages, communication, and finances. The conferences are usually held at a nice resort and are made as affordable as possible. There are often scholarships available. Information is available at your FCA state office.

Randy and I have attended eight Coach's Camps. Our first was in 1979 in Alamosa, Colorado. I'll have to admit I was a little uncomfortable because this was our first vacation away from our children, and we didn't know anyone. I remember standing in the cafeteria line with Nancy and Tom Osborne of Nebraska. What a thrill to see a high profile coaching family up close–as regular people, yet inspiring role models.

Later, when I asked Nancy for advice, she wrote me, "One of the decisions Tom and I made when our family was young was to set aside one night a week for Tom and me to have some time alone so we didn't lose touch with each other." She also said to plan how wins and losses would be handled, because you are sending a message to your children and the community. She added, "If you don't set your own course as a young family, the world will, and you will feel out of control...and you will be!"

Nancy, Lil Wacker, Donell Teaff, and many other wives of recognized coaches have been generous with their concern for coaches' wives at these conferences.

6. Special seminars for women by FCA

A unique and creative weekend seminar called "Feminar," was sponsored by FCA coaches' wives at Austin College and Sherman High School, in Sherman, Texas. The weekend included lively and inspirational speakers on women's issues, promotional T-shirts, and even a local FCA cookbook. What a great way for coaches' wives to share Jesus Christ with women in the community.

7. FCA can minister one on one.

Deborah Ford (University of Arkansas) tells of her experience:

"Sometimes being a coach's wife during a staff transition can be awkward. A short time after we lost the job at Clemson, Dal Shealy came to visit us. He also came to visit Coach Hatfield who had just been named the new head coach at Clemson. Dal was supporting Coach Hatfield but at the same time caring for us. During his visit, he told me how special the women were on the incoming staff and that I should meet them. I must say, on the inside of my heart I thought, 'You have got to be kidding.'

"Coach Hatfield had kept a close friend's husband on his staff. A few weeks later, my friend had a luncheon for the new wives and she included me. Two of these women became dear friends of mine. One was in a Moms-in-Touch group in my home and the other was in a Bible study with me in my church. God used these women in a mighty way to heal my hurts and show me how the body of Christ is greater than any circumstances.

"I have thought of those years many times and realize, left to myself, I could have missed the lessons and blessings God intended for me. But by His grace, I now can hold on to the promise that he uses all things for my good and His glory."

Ours is a unique sisterhood and ministry. Allow the Lord to use you in the FCA mission field. The athletes are watching and noticing *you* as well as your husband.

We Need Each Other

As you close this book, I hope you feel that you've spent time with many new friends. Coaches' wives need each other. I appreciate the wisdom and honesty of those who responded to the survey. It has been a privilege for me to relate their experiences. However, no book about coaches' wives is complete without your story!

Coaches and wives need each other, too. The coaching life will have its share of ups and downs. But if you lean into your challenges, and if you "team up" with your husband, you will *always win*. You might even be accused of having a *home field advantage!*

Appendix

Special thanks to all the wives that helped contribute information to this book . . .

Leslie Baca	Bastrop H. S., TX
Laura Barber	West Mesquite H. S., TX
Brenda Beasley	Houston King H. S., TX
Pam Bethea	Stephenville H. S., TX
Kathy Boyd	Hawkins H. S., TX
Marihelen Boyd	Harlingen H. S., TX
Christy Brink	Plains H. S.,TX
Leigh Bruno	Katy H. S.,TX
Charlotte Bruster	Abilene, TX
Trish Brymer	San Antonio Kirby Jr. Hi., TX
Catherine Bundick	Abilene Cooper H. S.,TX
Cindy Campbell	Texas Tech University
Jenny Castellaw	Duncanville H. S.,TX
Jonlyn Castillo	Abilene Cooper H. S.,TX
Diane Christiansen	Eastern Oregon State, OR
Maxine Clark	Venus H. S.,TX
Patricia Clyde	Overton H. S.,TX
Lisa Coleman	Odessa Permian H. S.,TX
Brenda Conley	Menard H. S.,TX
Susan Cook	Longview H. S.,TX
Marcia Couch	Abilene Cooper H. S.,TX
Monica Criswell	Bryan H. S.,TX
Philda Dudgeon	Throckmorton H. S.,TX
Doenye Essary	Navasota H. S.,TX
Karen Evans	Menard H. S.,TX
Judy Everett	New Braunfels Canyon H. S.,TX
Nancy Fleener	San Antonio Jefferson H. S.,TX
Deborah Ford	University of Arkansas
Stephanie Gage	Lewisville H. S.,TX
Darline Graves	San Augustine H. S.,TX
Bonnie Green	Bryan H. S.,TX
Judy Gregory	West Point Military Academy, NY

Linda Griffin	White Oak H. S.,TX
Diane M. Hale	Bloomsburg University, PA
Beverly Harkness	Crosby H. S.,TX
Laurie Harper	Dallas, TX
JoSarah Harrell	Little Cypress-Mauriceville H. S.,TX
Kathy Harrell	Ennis H. S.,TX
Rebecca Hixon	Wake Forest University, NC
Donna Hoffman	Shepherd H. S.,TX
Sandy Horne	Valparaiso University, IN
Maureen Huber	Warsah H. S., Indiana
Michelle Hugg	Allef Elsik H. S.,TX
Angela Jackson	Valley Mills H. S.,TX
Kaye Jones	Pilot Point H. S.,TX
Mary Joseph	Texas High School Coaches Association, Austin, TX
Susan Keeling	Hardin-Simmons University, TX
Donna Killian	Florence H. S.,TX
Kim Kincaid	San Antonio Churchill H. S.,TX
Maureen Kyle	St. Ignatius H. S., OH
Pat Kyle	St. Ignatius H. S., OH
Joan Lawrence	Commerce H. S.,TX
Becky Leaf	Lubbock Monterey H. S.,TX
Sue Ledbetter	Southlake Carroll H. S.,TX
Kae Loerwald	Austin McNiel H. S.,TX
Donell Loyd	San Antonio Taft H. S.,TX
Kelle MacLeay	San Antonio Taft H. S.,TX
Arlene Macovic	University of Texas, TX
Ellie Mallory	Indiana University, IN
Vickie McQueen	Mason H. S.,TX
Marian Merritt	Montgomery H. S.,TX
Julia Lee Moore	Kerens H. S.,TX
Liz Mullins	Northwestern State, LA
Maura Nelson	San Antonio Churchill H. S.,TX
Ginny Norris	Adams State College, CO
Nancy Osborne	University of Nebraska, NE

Merry Parker	Cleburne H. S.,TX
Lynne Payne	Evensville Rhea Co. H. S.,TN
Sharron Perez	Round Rock H. S.,TX
Audra Perrin	Lewisville H. S.,TX
Lisa Phillips	Hardin-Simmons University, TX
Patti Phillips	Plano East H. S.,TX
Pat Poe	Irving ISD, TX
Janene Pratt	Bryan, TX
Leila Pruneda	McAllen Rowe H. S.,TX
Stacey Rhiddlehoover	McMurry University,TX
Cindy Rhodes	Timpson H. S.,TX
Phyllis Rogers	A & M Consolidaated H. S., TX
Kathy Rutledge	Converse Judson H. S.,TX
Sharon Sanderson	Celeste H. S.,TX
Jane Schwartz	Klein H. S.,TX
Frances "Cissy" Seyle	Hill AFB, UT
Barbara Shealy	FCA, Kansas City, MO
Jackie Sherwood	Lubbock ISD, TX
Melanie Simon	University of North Texas, TX
Yvonne Sinclair	Abilene, TX
Carolyn Slaughter	Ballinger H. S.,TX
Kelly H. Smith	Highland Park H. S.,TX
Sandy Sabock	University of Northern Illinois, IL
Loretta Sorrells	Greeneville H. S.,TN
Carol Sparks	Carson-Newman College, TN
Chris Steckel	Houston Oilers, TX
Teena Story	Wylie H. S.,TX
Janis Stregles	Vanston H. S.,TX
Trace Teaff	Dallas, TX
Karen Tucker	Clifton H. S.,TX
Jackie Van Wieren	Hope College, MI
Linda K. VanSant	Louise H. S.,TX
Lillian Wacker	University of Minnesota, MN
Becky Walker	San Antonio Churchill H. S.,TX
Carol Warren	Abilene H. S.,TX

Tara Wells	Abilene Cooper H. S.,TX
Julie West	Kemp H. S.,TX
Yollie Wilkins	Odessa Permian H. S. TX
Karen Wilson	Brownwood H. S.,TX
Katherine Wood	Brownwood H. S.,TX
Anne Young	Waxahachie H. S.,TX
Diane Young	University of Sioux Falls, SD

Bibliography

BOOKS

Bowden, Bobby and Smith, Bill. *More Than Just A Game*. Nashville: Thomas Nelson Publishers, 1994.

Courtet, Robert V. Jr. *Financial Planning for Coaches*, Robinson-Humphrey, Atlanta, Georgia, 1995.

Crosson, Russ. *A Life Well Spent*. Nashville: Thomas Nelson Publishers, 1994.

Dayton, Howard L. Jr. *Your Money: Frustration or Freedom*. Wheaton, Illinois: Tyndale House Publishers, 1979.

Dooley, Barbara. *Put Me In, Coach*. Longstreet Press, 1991.

Gray, John, Ph.D. *Mars and Venus in the Bedroom*, HarperCollins Publishers, 1995.

Goldsmith, Olivia and Collins, Amy Fine. *Simple Isn't Easy*. New York: Harper Collins Publishers, 1995.

Harley, Willard F. Jr. *Love Busters*. Grand Rapids: Fleming Revell and Co., 1992.

Harley, Willard F. Jr. *His Needs, Her Needs*. Grand Rapids: Fleming Revell and Co., 1986.

Klauser, Henriette Anne. *Put Your Heart on Paper*. New York: Bantam Books, 1995.

Landry, Tom. *Tom Landry: An Autobiography*. New York: Zondervan Publishing, 1990.

McDonald, Gail. *High Call, High Privilege*. Wheaton, Illinois: Tyndale House Publishers, Inc., 1981.

Miller, Susan. *After the Boxes are Unpacked.* Colorado Springs, Co: Focus on the Family Publishing, 1995.

Smalley, Gary and Trent, John. *The Blessing.* Nashville: Thomas Nelson Publishing, 1986.

Phelps, Teresa Godwin. *The Coach's Wife–A Notre Dame Memoir.* W. W. Norton & Co. Publishers, 1994.

Poynter, Dan and Bingham, Mindy. *Is There A Book Inside You?* Santa Barbara, CA: Para Publishing, 1992.

Rainey, Dennis. *Staying Close.* Dallas: Word Publishing, 1992.

Truman, Margaret. *First Ladies.* New York: Random House, 1995.

Winning Seasons. American Football Coaches' Wives Association, c/o Adcraft, 7108 Fairway Drive, Palm Beach Gardens, Florida 33418.

NEWSLETTERS

"Behind The Bench." Fellowship of Christian Athletes. 8701 Leeds Road, Kansas City, MO 64129-1680.

Shaffner, Donna. "The Support Staff" American Football Coaches' Wives Association, 522 Raub Street, Easton, PA 18042.

TAPES

Ortlund, Anne and Ray. "Sex In A Growing Marriage." Renewal Ministries, 4500 Campus Drive, Suite 662, Newport Beach, CA 92660.

Kirby, Andrea. "Winning with the Media." Andrea Kirby Coaches Inc., 510 Waverly Stree, Palo Alto, CA 94301, 1-800-831-3883.